THE DECISION

NAKITA ROWELL-STEVENS

Rowell-Stevens, Nakita. *The Decision* Copyright © 2021 by Nakita Rowell-Stevens

Published by KWE Publishing: www.kwepub.com

ISBN 978-1-956092-04-2

First Edition. All rights reserved. No portion of this book may be reproduced, stored in a retrieval system, or transmitted in any form or by any means — including by not limited to electronic, mechanical, digital, photocopy, recording, scanning, blogging or other — except for brief quotations in critical reviews, blogs, or articles, without the prior written permission of the authors.

To Christine Hasbrouck, thank you for offering your cozy bed & breakfast, The Grey Swan Inn, to me while I finished this book.

"**Ms. Cooper, the conference room** will be ready for your meeting in 20 minutes."

"Thank you, Elise. Please tell my team to meet me there at 10:30, and to come ready with their ideas for our upcoming campaign."

"Will do, Ms. Cooper."

I sit back in the soft, leather chair of my twelve hundred-square-foot office. I remember when my apartment was smaller than this. Looking outside at the lake, I revel in the beauty of the emerging spring season. I love spring. It symbolizes new birth, new beginnings, and growth. I feel like I've experienced all four seasons in my life, and finally, I'm in full bloom. Just a few years ago, I was navigating through the rough, frigid winter of my own life.

How did I get here?

Eight years ago, I had meager expectations for my life. Right after high school graduation, I learned I was pregnant, not the glowing news you want to tell your parents when they have all these big dreams of you going to college, getting your dream job and making a pile of money. Fact is, college wasn't a part of my plan. For me, high school was a social club. When it came to the academics, I found myself unmotivated and bored. While my parents wanted me to do well and encouraged me, they weren't exactly the picture of success. My dad worked the night shift in the local steel mill and my mom was a supervisor at the main supermarket by day. I grew up in a small, rural town in North Carolina so there weren't many shining examples of success to spur me on.

Once I graduated from school, I tried to prepare myself for early motherhood. My boyfriend was relatively supportive, but we were young, so he struggled with handling the new responsibility of becoming a father. Our primitive culture firmly believed you get pregnant, you get married. However, we both realized that was not what we wanted because, quite honestly, we were too young to know what we wanted. Though we were about to become parents, getting married wasn't the answer for us. I liked Zack, hell, maybe even loved him, but I wasn't ready to make a lifelong commitment at the tender age of 18.

So, we found a way to make it work. I gave birth to a beautiful baby girl, and we named her Jasmine. My mom helped me secure a position at the market, working 40-50 hours a week. It didn't take long for me to realize this was not the life I wanted. Zack found himself working at the steel mill with my dad. Déjà vu started kicking in big time. If I didn't do anything to break the chain, Zack and I would become my parents. While I love both of my parents very much, I wanted more than our small town could offer. I had dreams of a corporate career, working in a big high-rise building with glass panels. My home town didn't have that. Something had to change.

One of my friends from high school moved to Atlanta after graduation. She was always texting me and telling me how great it was and how much opportunity there was in the city. Dreams of flashing city lights haunted me every night. Her description of life in the city was spellbinding. I decided to give her a call and ask a huge favor. A dutiful friend, Allison allowed me and my daughter, Jasmine, to crash at her apartment while I enrolled in a local community college and searched for a job. I can never repay her for getting me started on a solid career path so that I could earn a decent living. When I decided to move, I asked Zack to come with me, so that we could raise our daughter together. His obligation to his mom and dad kept him in North Carolina. His father was a disabled veteran and his mother only worked part-time, so he felt a need to take care of them. He urged me to move to Atlanta without him, knowing it was best for me and Jasmine. He promised to fulfill his obligations as her father and come down to visit every couple of months.

After enrolling in college, I discovered a real flair for art and design. I transferred to The Art Institute where I earned my bachelor's in graphic design. I finally felt like I was moving forward in my life. I worked odd end jobs part-time to pay for Jasmine's food and diapers. Allison refused to accept rent from me. She said getting to hang out with a cute kid like Jasmine, and knowing she was helping us get on our feet was payment enough.

Shortly after graduating college, Allison was able to help me land an entry-level full-time graphic designer position at the advertising firm where she worked. After working for them a few months,

I was able to move out of Allison's place and get my own apartment where Jasmine could have her own room.

I started working my way up the corporate ladder and just three short years ago, I was offered the creative director position at the agency. Zack has been good for his word and spends time with Jasmine every couple of months. He's a great father. When I think of where I started and where I am today, I should be proud of what I've accomplished. Life is pretty is good – at least I think so.

"Great brainstorming session, guys! I think we have some solid ideas to present to the client on Thursday. Elise, will you please email me the notes and we'll get together on Monday to work on the presentation?"

She nods in agreement as she exits the conference room.

I gather my things in the conference room while the rest of my creative team exits to their respective work areas. Allison stays behind. After starting at the agency as an entry level designer, the President saw my talent and immediately put me on the fast track for management. Now Allison is my team lead for all web design campaigns. When I look up, she is just standing there, looking at me with this goofy smile on her face.

"What are you smiling at?" I challenge her.

She walks over and places her arms around me.

"I'm just so proud of you," she says. "You've been through a lot. I know, because I've been there with you, and look at you now. You're my boss."

"Yeah, it's funny," I snicker. "I've been in this role for three years now. Ten years ago, I thought I'd be ringing up groceries with my mom back home and that would be all she wrote. It's definitely been a journey."

"I'm just so glad you got out of that place," Allison sighs. "That place is just too small to make a decent living. I'm glad you took the risk and moved away, even though it meant leaving Zack behind."

I lean back, thinking of Zack.

"Zack is a great father, even from a distance. At heart, he's an old country boy with roots back home. He could never part with his family. They rely on him too much and he'd never want to leave them in a lurch. I can't fault him for that. I also know that our daughter deserves more than small town living can offer, and he agrees, which I am thankful for. Not many fathers would be so understanding."

I get up and wrap Allison in a bear hug.

"And, I'm glad you took me in and gave me a chance to start a new life with Jasmine."

"How's she doing, by the way?" she asks.

"Amazing," I beam. "I'm so proud of her. Getting straight A's in school, which is way better than I ever did. Zack always encourages her and helps her with her homework via video chat, which she loves. And, Zack has been so great about my relationship with Tony. At first, I wasn't sure how he was going to react, with another man around his daughter, but he has given me no grief about it at all. He said he just wants us both to be happy."

"That's awesome, Talia!" Allison grins. "Things are looking up. Great kid. Great job. A great man in your life. What else could you possibly ask for?"

I plaster on an artificial smile.

"I guess you're right," I say, "this is it. I've made it. What else could I ask for?"

Allison and I both leave the conference room to work in our respective offices. For the rest of the afternoon, I find myself lost in my thought, daydreaming about my life and what it has become. Before I know it, it is 5:30. As fun as my job can be, things are becoming routine, mundane even. I get up, get Jasmine off to school, go to work, get off at 5:00 and then it starts all over again. But, that's normal, right? That's what life is about. Before I can ponder this further, my boss, Mr. Stevens, interrupts my thoughts with a tap on my door which is ajar.

"Talia!" He pokes his head in cautiously.

"Yes," I snap out of my trance.

"I'm so glad you're still here" he says, sounding relieved, "I really need to talk to you about something. Can you meet me in my office in about five minutes?"

"Of course," I respond, feeling a little anxious.

"Good."

Perplexed, he turns on his heels before leaving, "I'm not interrupting anything, am I? Any important deadlines you need to finish up?"

"No, of course not."

He gives me a curt nod and leaves my office.

I've been doing a good job, right? I wonder what the sense of urgency is. He's not going to fire me, is he?

As I walk from my office toward his, I notice a few colleagues lingering behind in their cubes, working hard on their individual campaigns.

I slowly poke my head into Mr. Stevens' office.

"Mr. Stevens?"

"Talia," he smiles, "come on in. And, it's been nearly four years. We're not strangers. Call me Tim. I'm not into all of the formalities."

His spirits seem high. I take this as a good sign.

He gets up from behind his over-sized mahogany desk, and closes the door to the office. I feel the mood in the room shift. He's serious now.

Uh-oh.

Instead of walking back behind his desk, he sits in the chair right beside me.

His warm smile immediately relieves the growing tension in my gut.

"Talia, are you happy here?"

Not exactly what I was expecting to hear from him.

"Of course, Mr. Stevens, I mean Tim," I answer nervously. "This is the best job I've ever had. I love it here!"

"That's great to hear, Talia," he says, "and you can relax, this is a good meeting. I love having you here as well and think you have done a tremendous job in the three years you have been working as our creative director. Our clients couldn't be happier with the quality of work that you're putting out for their campaigns, which is the reason why I wanted to talk to you this evening."

Tim gets up and starts pacing the floor.

"It's hard to believe but Bradley and I started this company almost fifteen years ago. When we started the business in our small, 800-square-foot apartment, I don't think we ever thought it would blossom into the agency it is today. We've gone from just the two of us to 150 employees over the years. And, my vision for this place is still expanding. I see us growing to 300 employees and opening more offices in the next five years. Bradley and I have been friends and business partners for a long time, but about a month ago, he informed that he had other business interests that he wanted to pursue and that he will slowly be abdicating his responsibilities here over the next year. That's where you come in, Talia."

He takes a labored sigh before continuing.

"I understand that you have only been with the company for a few years, and I normally would not approach anyone with that short of a tenure with an opportunity like this, but I really like you, Talia. I love your fight and your vision, and you've already proven yourself to be a valuable asset to our leadership team. I need someone to partner with me to take this company to the next level. Your expertise in the creative division has been impeccable. Now, I want to challenge you to more. I'd like to take you under my wing as our new executive vice president. I understand that this will require you taking on some additional responsibilities above and beyond your role of creative director, like working with our account management team and looking at our revenue and cash flow on accounts and new business. But I think you're fully capable. I've already discussed this with Bradley and he fully agrees with me on this as well."

He pauses, observing the bewildered look on my face. *My God, I haven't even been here a full four years!*

"Talia, I don't want you to make any decisions in haste. I realize that I've just dropped a lot on you, and if you think it is too much, that is perfectly fine. I want you in this role, but I will respect and value you just as much if you tell me that you'd like to continue in your role as creative director with the agency. But…I think you can serve the agency much better in this capacity."

I try to speak but no words come out. Sensing my hesitation, Tim walks behind his desk, opens up a drawer and pulls out an envelope.

Reaching over the desk, he hands the envelope to me.

"Here," he says, "I would not ask you to take on such a big

responsibility with our agency without adequate compensation. This envelope includes the full details of my offer. Take some time to review and then get back to me. There is no rush to make this decision. I want you to think it over and come back to me with any questions. Take a couple weeks if you need to."

I take the envelope. It feels heavy in my hand, as if it holds my entire future inside.

Searching for oxygen, I am finally able to muster a response.

"Th-thank you, Tim, for this opportunity, and for believing in me enough to even consider me for something like this. I must admit, I'm shocked. Aren't there other employees on your staff more qualified for this role than me?"

Tim sits down behind his desk again, folds his arms, and leans back in deep thought.

"We have some very talented people here, yes. But there is a difference between talent and vision. I find that a lot of my employees' lack vision. I need someone who can see the potential of what can be, and then make it real. I feel that you do that with our clients all the time when you're working on a campaign. It's one of your finest qualities and I want to expand that to serve our company on a bigger level. So, to answer your question, no, there is no one more qualified for this role than you. Yes, there are people with more tenure, but that does not necessarily make them qualified. Does that make sense?"

"Yes," I reply, clinging tightly to the envelope in my hand. "I guess I'm a little concerned about what others will think of me taking on a position like this when I've only been here a short time."

Tim gives me a stern look.

"Talia Cooper," he scolds, "one of the first things you need to learn as a leader of this company is to stop worrying about what others think of you. That is none of your concern. Your job is to do what is best for the company. Yes, feelings may be hurt because there are people who have been here longer that may think they deserve this position. But, make no mistake, you are the most qualified person for the job - period. That is, if you choose to take it."

I ponder his words.

"I don't want to hold you up any longer. It's almost 6:30 and I know you have to get home to that little girl of yours. Take some time and think this over."

I stand up, lean over and extend my hand.

"Thank you. I still don't know what I did to deserve this, but I appreciate you thinking of me."

Tim surprises me when he walks around his desk and wraps me in an embrace.

"You can do this, now get out of here."

I leave his office, mesmerized by what just happened. I don't remember how I get from the office to my car, I'm so dumbfounded. What a day! I drive home in silence. My mind is all over the place. I woke up this morning feeling like something might be missing in my life, but I couldn't put my finger on what that was. And now this!

I recall my earlier conversation with Allison. I do have a great life, but why do I feel like something is missing? She is right. I have a great job. A great man. A great kid. What else could I possibly want? Could this new opportunity that Tim just presented fill this gap? I need to clear my head. I don't want to think about this anymore today. I just need to get home, squeeze my daughter tight and tell her I love her. Tonight is game night with Jasmine and Tony, a welcome distraction. We always have so much fun.

Leaving the weight of the day behind me, I open the door to my 3,000-square-foot townhome.

"Mommy," Jasmine squeals as she rushes the door to jump into my arms. Gosh, that feels good.

"Hey sweet pea," I squeeze her back and give her a kiss, "how was your day?"

My daughter goes into an excited rant about her day, while I place my envelope on the kitchen table and give her my full attention.

"Where's Kelly?"

"She's in the living room," Jasmine responds. Playing with my hair before I sit her back on the floor, she asks, "Is Tony coming over for game night tonight?"

"You know it," I say, "and you get to pick the game. Why don't you work on that now?"

Jasmine scurries into the other room, rifling through our game collection. I catch up with the babysitter to pay her and get a quick update.

Kelly gathers her things.

"Thank you for staying a little late with her today," I say, "my boss needed me to meet with him a little longer than I expected."

"No problem," Kelly responds, "Jaz is a great kid. I don't mind the extra time. She's finished up all her homework and she's excited about game night."

"She really enjoys it." I take off my blazer and settle on the couch.

Kelly says a quick good night and she is gone. For a moment, there is complete silence, except for Jasmine rummaging through the games in the other room. I can tell she might be a while, so I lay back on the couch and bask in a few minutes of serenity. I can't help but wonder what's in that envelope. Is it the answer to the hollow feeling I'd been experiencing lately? Wait, I said I was not going to think about this anymore tonight, so I resolve to push those thoughts out of my head for now and just enjoy the quiet.

"I need a spa day." I whisper to myself.

The sound of the doorbell interrupts my meditative state.

"I got it!" Jasmine races to the front door.

"Ask who it is first," I command. I know it's Tony but have been training Jasmine not to just open the door to anyone when the doorbell rings. I sit up on the couch and listen intently.

"Who is it?" she asks, playfully. She knows it's Tony.

Playing her game, he answers, "The pizza man."

"Pizza?" Jasmine jumps up and down excitedly, "Mommy?" she looks at me her big brown eyes, asking for permission to open the door.

I nod my approval and she opens the door.

"Hey there, kiddo," Tony scoops Jasmine up in one arm, while holding two pizzas in the other.

I walk over and rescue the pizzas from his grip and sit them on the kitchen table.

"You're impossible," I shake my head.

"You're incredible," he responds as he releases my ever eager nine-year-old, as she races to the kitchen, to dig into her favorite dinner.

"Pizza!"

As I walk over to calm Jasmine's excitement before she rips into the pizza box, I feel Tony's strong arms wrap around my waist and pull me toward him.

"Just where do you think you're going?" He asks as he lands a passionate kiss on my lips that leaves me breathless.

This man gets my heart racing. He is not only good with me, but he is good with my kid. And to me…that counts the most. As far as looks are concerned, I certainly can't complain. Dark, tanned complexion, dark hair, and green eyes, Tony is eye candy. He's smart too. He is an architect at one of the top firms in town. We've been dating for about eight months now, and things have been starting to get serious. We recently started doing game night with Jasmine about two months ago, and she looks forward to it every week. Jasmine loves him. I'm pretty sure I do, too.

"What's going on in that pretty little head of yours?" Tony surmises.

Damn, lost in my thoughts again.

I grab a plate and a slice of pizza.

"Honestly, I was thinking how lucky I am to have that special little girl over there, and you."

Tony plants a tender kiss on my forehead, before reaching around and grabbing a slice of pizza for himself.

"I love you, too," he responds.

I smile affectionately. I know he means those words. I haven't reciprocated yet; part of me feels like it's implied but, I've been too afraid to say it out loud. The remarkable thing about him is he hasn't pressured me at all about it. He just loves me all the same.

After wolfing down her pizza and giving me and Tony five whole minutes of silence, Jasmine is ready to play.

Wide-eyed brown expectant eyes look at me and then Tony, "Game night?"

"Game night it is," Tony affirms. "What game are we playing tonight?"

Jasmine grabs Tony's hand and leads him into the den.

"Come see."

Realizing that I'm still in my work clothes, I head toward the stairs, "I'm going to go change. You guys go ahead and set up and I'll be down in just a minute."

I double back to grab the envelope off the kitchen counter.

As I'm changing into some comfortable jeans, I find myself fixated on the envelope that is now sitting on my dresser, wondering what is waiting for me inside. I want to open it up so badly but resist the urge to do so until the night is over. Game night has become a big deal for Jasmine, and I want to honor that. Tonight is family time.

There were several other boyfriends before Tony, and none even came close to measuring up to him. I had to build my personal self-image up to the point that I even felt I was worthy of a guy like Tony, and for a while that was a problem. I found myself dating a lot of jerks and I think Jasmine could see right through them before I could. Now, everything was different. Tony is all I could ever ask for in a guy. Allison was right. What else could I possibly want or need now?

"Hey, what's on your mind? You look lost in thought." Tony had come upstairs to check on me. "We were starting to wonder where you'd run off to. You ready? Jasmine has the game all picked out."

"Yes, I'm ready."

Tony stares at me analytically.

"You okay?" he says, "something is distracting you. You want to talk about it?"

I touch Tony's arm gently, reassuring him that everything is okay.

"I'm fine. Jasmine will have both of our heads if we don't get our butts downstairs and play with her. What game did she pick out?"

Tony grabs my arm and starts to lead me out of the bedroom, skeptical.

"Her favorite, Monopoly," he says, never averting his gaze.

"Of course, it's her favorite," I say, trying to slide past Tony's large frame, "because it goes on forever."

Tony slips his arms around my waist.

"This conversation is not over young lady. Something's going on with you, and I intend to find out exactly what it is."

Tony is persistent, a quality I love about him. I just don't know if I am ready to talk to him about something I'm still sorting out in my own head. I wrap my fingers around his and lead him downstairs.

"Later. Jasmine is waiting for us."

※

After a three-hour bout of Monopoly, complete with cookies and milk, it is time to tuck my little munchkin in. Since it is past her bedtime, she drifts off quickly. I shut the light off, and as I'm about to shut her door, Jasmine's sleepy voice stops me.

"Mommy?"

"Yes, sweetheart," I hurry to her bedside.

"I really like our game nights."

Running my hands over her disheveled hair, I kiss her temple, "I know, sweetie."

"I really like, Tony, too." She pauses for a moment, as if she's choosing her next words carefully. "Maybe you should marry him."

I almost fall off her bedside. I knew she liked Tony, but marriage was far from my mind. I haven't even told him those three magic words yet, although I'm pretty sure I do. Still, though, marry him?!

"You-you think Tony and I should get married?"

Jasmine smiles, her sleepy eyes widen slightly. There's wisdom in those brown eyes way beyond her years. She's an old soul.

"I know you really like him, Mom. I can tell. And, if I was going to have another dad, I'd be OK with it being him."

"Well that's good to know, kiddo. You have no idea how much it means that you like him so much. But let's cross that bridge when we get to it, OK?"

I plant one more goodnight kiss on her forehead, and she closes her eyes.

Closing the door to her the bedroom, I shake my head. She thinks we should get married.

"What are you smiling about?" Tony is in the kitchen pouring a glass of wine when I come downstairs.

"That daughter of mine," I say as I snatch his glass for myself.

"What did she do now?" Tony smirks at my thievery and begins to pour a second glass.

"You should know, she definitely approves of you."

"It's good to have her approval. She can be a tough critic," Tony grins.

"Then, she told me that it was okay with her if we wanted to get married."

Tony's smile fades to a more serious expression.

"What did you say to that?" He poses.

"I told her that I was glad that she liked you, and that we'd just cross that bridge when we get to it."

Closing the gap between us, Tony walks around the kitchen island toward me.

"Where exactly are we?" He inquires.

Immediately out of my comfort zone, I back away.

"I-I don't know."

"You don't know? We've been dating for eight months, and you don't know?" He pulls me closer before I can run away. "I think you know exactly where we are. You're just afraid to say it."

My heart is racing, and my cheeks are flushed.

Wrapping his arms around me like a padlock, he demands an answer. "Say it."

"Wh-what?" I pretend I don't know what he wants, but I do. I know exactly what he wants, and I know the answer.

I turn my gaze away from him, and he gently turns it back.

"Say it," he whispers, his soft breath tickling my ear.

I know exactly what I'm feeling. I can't deny it. I don't know why it is so hard to express my feelings. Be courageous, Talia. Nothing bad can come of this. I look him in the eyes and tell him how I feel.

"I love you."

A weight lifts off my shoulders with those words. The funny thing is, I can tell by the expression on Tony's face that it pleases him, but his expression is not one of relief. He already knows how I feel; he just wanted to hear me say the words.

Kissing me on the lips as a reward for my honesty, he says, "See, now, how hard was that?"

Relishing his embrace, I realize that it isn't hard at all, loving him.

"I guess it wasn't that hard." I realize that I've just taken a first step at breaking down some of the walls I've built up to protect my heart. Zack was the first man that I ever loved and leaving him was more painful that I've ever been willing to admit. Opening my heart to another man has not been easy.

Pulling away, Tony sits down at the kitchen table and gestures for me to join him.

"Now that we know where we stand with each other, and we're in the habit of openly sharing our feelings, we've got something else to talk about."

I join him at the table, curious.

"We do?"

Leaning across the table, he takes my hands in his. "Yes. I know something is bothering you, and I want to know what it is. Several times tonight, I've noticed you going off to la-la land. And, quite honestly, it hasn't just been tonight. I've noticed you spacing out like this for weeks now and you just keep telling me that everything is fine. Are you going to tell me what's really going on with you?"

Leaning back in my chair, I ponder how I can explain what is going on with me when I don't even understand it myself. Running my hands across my face, I respond, "It's complicated."

Tony is not satisfied with my answer.

"Enlighten me."

"It's not an excuse, Tony. I'm having a difficult time trying to figure things out on my own, so it's hard to articulate," I defend.

"What things are you trying to figure out?" He questions.

I search for the right words to express what I am feeling. "What my purpose is in this life. What I should be doing?"

Tony looks perplexed.

"Are you not happy? I thought you were in a good place. Things have been going well at the job lately, right? You've come so far, working your way up to creative director? I thought you loved your job. What's missing?"

Tears begin to well up in my eyes, and I'm not even sure why.

"That's just it. I don't know yet what's missing. I can't imagine what could be missing from my life right now, but it's just a feeling, and I can't shake it. I told you it's complicated."

Tony pushes his chair back from the table and pats his lap for me to join him. Taking his cue, I get up and sit on his lap and he circles his arms around me.

"What are you feeling?"

"Like...like something is missing. I have an amazing job, and I'm great at it, but I just don't feel fulfilled anymore, which doesn't make sense because I've worked so hard to get where I am. Why would I be unfulfilled? I should be happy, right?"

Stroking my hair, Tony replies, "Maybe you're just in a rut. It happens to all of us in our careers from time to time. It's not uncommon. I've even felt that way before in my career."

His words plant a glimmer of hope. "You did? How did you move past it? What did you do?"

"It was a while ago, not long after I'd graduated college. I was just getting started as a young architect. I studied design architecture, so I worked closely with a junior designer. Because of my lack of experience, it left much to be desired. I wasn't an intern, but I felt like an errand boy. I was young and ambitious and ready for the advanced stuff. I didn't feel like I was doing what I needed to be doing, like I was wasting my talents in a dead-end job. I wanted to quit."

Perking up, I ask, "What did you do? Did you quit that job to find something more challenging?"

"No, I didn't," Tony surprises me with his response. "I talked to a guy at the company who was a senior level designer, working in the area I wanted to be in. I told him my frustrations and how I felt unchallenged in my role. He reassured me that I was just going through what every new architect experiences after graduating college. We all want the grand career, but we must start at the bottom to get where we want to go. It's a vetting process, to rule out the weak. He told me to be patient and prove myself where I was, and I would make it. So, that's what I did. It wasn't easy. I wasn't happy every step of the way, but I kept my eye on the bigger goal moved up in my position to where I wanted to be. Now, I'm a senior designer and I get to mentor those new guys that were like me when they first started out, frustrated and unsure of their new role."

I get up and sit in a chair next to Tony.

"Are you happy now? Was it worth it to wait those years to get where you are? Do you feel fulfilled now?" I'm desperate for answers.

"Well, yeah. I like my job. And, honestly, even if I didn't, I don't know if it would be worth it to sacrifice the years of investment I've put into this career."

This conversation is making me even more confused about my own situation. I can appreciate Tony's perspective, but I'm not sure we are on the same page.

"You're saying, even if you weren't happy, you'd stay?" I blink twice, trying to absorb what he's telling me.

"Yea, I guess so," he responds.

I'm not satisfied with his answer, and it shows. Tony grabs my hand and begins to caress it.

"Talia, I like my job. More importantly, it provides a good, stable income. An income that can support my future wife and family," he explains.

My heart starts to race, as his gaze holds mine.

"You already know how I feel about you, and after some coaxing, tonight, you finally admitted how you feel about me. And, that little girl upstairs means the world to me. I don't know if you realize it or not, but I want to build a life with you - a great life, a stable life."

"Tony, I do love you. And, I see that for us, too. I've never been this happy. That's why this feeling I've been battling is so confusing, and then today..." My voice trails off.

"Today, what?" He asks.

Hesitating before continuing, I clear my throat.

"Today, Mr. Stevens made me an offer."

A sly grin spreads across Tony's face.

"What kind of offer?"

"A promotion."

"Well, that's great!" Tony replies. "What exactly did he offer you? More money?"

"He wants me to be a partner."

Jumping up from his seat in excitement, he scoops me up out of the chair into his arms.

"Oh, my God, Talia, that's great!" he screams.

"Shhh" I admonish, "you're going to wake Jasmine."

"I'm sorry. I'm sorry," he whispers, putting me down. "It's just...this is great news."

I wonder to myself, if it is so great, why is he more excited than I am? Shouldn't I feel this excited? What's wrong with me?

Tony notices that I am not celebrating with him. "You're not excited about this?"

"I don't know. I should be excited, right? It's a wonderful opportunity."

"Of course, it is! Isn't this what we work for our entire careers?" he asks.

Not knowing the answer to his question, I shrug, "I don't know. Is it?"

Tony looks at me like I have two heads.

"Yes...yes, Talia. This is it! You're there." Gesturing toward the ceiling, "There's nowhere else to go. You've reached the top."

So, there is a such thing as a glass ceiling. Even as great as this job offer is, I don't like the idea that I have nowhere to go from here.

Tony clutches my shoulders.

"This is a good thing," he says. "Stop stressing about this. You may feel overwhelmed because it is still new to you. Sleep on it, and we'll talk about it tomorrow. Are we still on for dinner tomorrow night, just you and me?"

"Yeah, Kelly is coming over to watch Jasmine."

Looking at his watch, Tony jumps up and grabs his coat. "My God, it's almost midnight. I've got an early morning meeting."

He leans in for a quick kiss.

"Let's talk more about this tomorrow, okay? Everything is going to be fine. Relish this moment. You should be on top of the world right now."

And with a big smile still on his face, he is out the door.

I walk into my living room and sink into my couch. What am I going to do? I'm so lost. I thought talking to Tony about this would help, but it just made it worse. Telling me that this partnership is the ceiling on my career leaves a sour feeling in the pit of my stomach. My fear is that if I'm already feeling empty and lost with this offer on my lap, what can I expect of my future? I want to feel alive and excited again.

When I was in college, I remember my final project in one of my business courses. We had to come up with our own business ideas and develop a plan to go to market. I decided to open a clothing boutique. We went through the entire process of starting the business all the way to the grand opening. I'd never had so much fun in my life! I shopped the different distributors to determine what apparel and accessories I wanted to carry in my store. I had to market to the students at the college to convince them to come out to my grand opening.

Clothes and fashion have been my jam for as long as I can remember. When I started making decent money at the agency, I invested in my wardrobe. My closet is an endless sea of shoes. I love shoes! Jasmine once told me, "Mommy, you have so many clothes in here, it looks like a store."

That brings a smile to my face. Perhaps Jasmine saw something I didn't. But I love my job, right? I didn't open a store when I got out of college. I got a job. That's because that's what everyone told me to do. I feel like I've been doing what everyone told me to do my entire life, except for my decision to leave home with Jasmine and start a new life here in Atlanta. That decision was all me. Once I made that decision, I allowed other people to come back into my life and drive and dictate decisions for me - Allison, Tim, Tony. I don't even think they realize what they are doing; I didn't even realize it myself. I'm just doing what I'm supposed to be doing, right?

According to Tony, I'm more than on track for where I should be in life. He said he would stay where he was, even if he wasn't happy - for the stability. So, I guess stability is the answer in life. If I take this partner position, my career will be stable. I mean, I'll be the boss - essentially.

Then I'll be giving up some of the aspects of my job I like, to take on more operational duties. Not taking this position will mean that I stay where I am, stagnant and not moving forward anymore - forever? Stability is important. I have a daughter to provide for after all. I want her to go to college and have a better start at life than I did. Without the stability of the income I make now, I can't promise her that. Tony and I have a real shot at a future together, so I know that he will partner with me to provide that stability for Jasmine. Of course, Zack wants the best for her, too, so he'll continue to be the best daddy for her and give her what she needs. Okay, then stability it is. I have a responsibility to my daughter and if that means that I'm a bit uncomfortable with where I am in my career, I'm just going to have to suck it up.

I get up and slowly walk upstairs. I peek in on my sleeping angel. She is certainly worth any and all sacrifices I have to make to give her the world. I close her door and walk into my room.

The envelope on my dresser is staring at me, begging to be opened. Haunted by it, I go into my bathroom to freshen up, and then into my closet to change into my pajamas. Enamored by my own wardrobe, I look around at all the fancy designer labels - clothes I could never afford just a few short years ago. Michael Kors. Prada. Gucci. Kate Spade. I love Kate Spade!

Dresses, suits and shoes, oh my! I feel like Carrie in *Sex in the City*. It feels good to be able to buy whatever I want freely. It feels good to live under my own roof. It feels good not to have to give Jasmine the old excuse, "I'm sorry honey, we can't do that now."

I glance at the dreaded envelope perched on my dresser. How can such a small thing hold so much power over me?

Picking it up, I sit on my plush, king-sized bed, and open it. There are two sheets of paper inside. The first letter reads:

Dear Talia Cooper:

Your performance with the agency as its creative director over the last three years has proved impeccable. Our client retention has improved 35% since you've started with us. Clearly, you were a great hire. We see even greater potential with you in this agency and would like to present a rare and unique opportunity to you.

Bradley and I began this agency over fifteen years ago. We've built it to extreme heights that we never imagined. Bradley has recently decided to phase himself out of the agency to pursue other interests, which leaves an opening for a new partner with the agency. I, on the other hand, have very ambitious goals to grow this agency nationwide and further increase our presence and impact in the advertising world. You possess the talent and ability to help me achieve this goal. I believe, partnered together, we can take this agency to the next level. I understand that you do not have years of experience in management, but you have talent and vision and I admire that in my employees. I will mentor you through this process, so you will not be alone. I will also invest in executive management training to acclimate you to your new role.

You have already proven to be a tremendous asset to this organization. I feel that you can contribute even more as my partner. While you will take on the role as my partner, your title will be vice president and you will not assume any fiscal responsibility for the agency. That burden will stay with Bradley and me. You will, however, receive a handsome compensation package above and beyond your current $95,000 annual salary as our creative director. Please see our full offer with compensation details enclosed along with the deadline for acceptance.

Also, this position has not been publicized throughout the company, so please refrain from sharing anything before a decision is made by both parties.

We appreciate your contributions to the agency and eagerly await your response.

Sincerely,
Timothy Stevens

I turn to the next page to review the full offer:

The agency of Stevens & Schmick would like to formally offer Talia Cooper the position of Vice President. In this role, you will assume full partnership duties that include but are not limited to: operations management and budgeting, management of executive staff, overseeing all creative campaigns for clients and working side by side with partner, Tim Stevens to run agency.

Compensation Details:
• Salary: $175,000/year + annual bonuses based upon revenue goals to range up to $100,000.
• Company car service

•Company laptop, cell phone and tablet
•Wardrobe service
•Complimentary fitness stipend
•Corporate expense account
•Access to the corporate apartment in the city

Benefits will continue as they are, but company will pick up cost for health insurance premiums and you will be required to complete a full executive physical each year.

Please sign below to acknowledge your acceptance of this offer.

Signature

I pinch myself to see if I am dreaming. Is this for real? I'd be a fool not to accept this offer, right? I mean, it is amazing, especially considering that nine years ago when Jasmine was born, I was making $7.50 an hour. Talk about rags to riches.

Tony said we needed stability to build a family; this is more than stability. I can easily save for Jasmine's college with this salary. And, wardrobe service! Yes, please! I toss the papers aside and lay on my bed. Daydreaming, I can see Tony, Jasmine and me living in a big brick home with a pool. But something is still missing, I can feel it. How can an offer like this not be enough? It has to be enough. Who in their right mind would turn something like this down? Tony is right. It doesn't get any better than this. I can't aspire for more...or can I? Is there something else out there that I have yet to discover? What's stopping me from pulling the trigger on this amazing opportunity?

I just need to sleep on it. The stress of the day has made this overwhelming, and I have a lot to think about it. I put the pile of papers on my nightstand and snuggle underneath my plush down comforter.

Beep, beep, beep!

The obnoxious sound of my alarm shocks me out of the bed onto the hard, cold floor. I'd been sound asleep. Realizing it is

Friday and not yet the weekend, I pick myself off the floor and try to get it together. When I reach to turn the alarm off, the envelope and papers on my nightstand tumble to the floor.

As I pick them up, memories of the previous day flood my mind. It isn't a dream. I read through the offer again. It's real; this is happening - to me. I slept like a baby last night but I'm not any closer to a decision today. At least I have some time to think this over. Tim said he'd give me a couple of weeks, and I need all of it.

I go downstairs, brew my coffee and wake Jasmine to get her ready for school. Within a couple of hours, I am back in the office, sitting at my desk. While most Fridays can be rather frantic, today is calm. I don't have any deadlines, so I can work on my projects uninterrupted.

Knock, knock...

"Come in."

Elise, my assistant, walks into the office with a beautiful arrangement of multi-colored roses.

"What's that?" I inquire.

"These," she sits the arrangement on my desk, "are for you."

It isn't a special occasion. Why would I be getting flowers?

Elise lingers in my office, waiting for me to read the card.

"Well..." she prompts.

I lift the card from the arrangement:

To the woman I love - I love our game nights with Jasmine, the sparkle in your eyes when you smile and the way you crinkle your nose when you're confused. I love everything about you and me together. Thank you for opening up to me last night. I took that as a sign of growth in our relationship, which couldn't make me happier. Don't let those feelings you're having worry you. I know you'll do what's best, but remember, you're not in it alone. Together, we'll figure it out because we're a team. Can't wait to have dinner with you tonight and have you all to myself. - Love always, Tony.

I hand the card over to Elise so that she can read it.

She giggles and hands the card back to me.

"He makes you happy, I can tell. There's a glow about you since you've been together."

"I am happy." I gush. "He's a great guy, and I'm lucky to have him in my life."

"It doesn't hurt that he's smoking hot," Elise whistles approvingly.

I laugh out loud at her bold proclamation, "Yes, that he is."

"Well, I better get back to work." Elise scoots out of my office and closes the door.

I take in the scent of the roses on my desk. I wonder if I should go over my offer with him after dinner tonight. He's right, as a couple, we are a team, so I should be comfortable sharing anything with him. The only thing is, I already know what he is going to say. After last night, I know where he stands on this partnership. If I decide not to accept it, I don't know what the next step will be for me. At least, not yet.

There's another light rapping on my door.

"Come in." This time it's Allison.

"Hey there."

Perhaps she can offer some neutral advice on this subject. I can't share all the details since Tim specified not to speak to anyone, but she could offer some perspective. But, not here.

"You've been holed up in your office all day today," she observes.

"Yea, I guess I didn't even realize it. Things have been crazy around here the last couple of weeks with campaign deadlines and new launches. Today is the first time in a while where I've had some time to just catch up on some things without a deadline looming over my head. And, the team is busy working on a big presentation in a couple of weeks, so I haven't heard much from them today, except for you, dear friend. What's up?"

Allison takes a seat across from me.

"I just came in here to check on you."

I glance up at her thoughtfully from the pile of papers on my desk.

"Thanks. I'm doing fine. By the way, what are you doing tomorrow night? Tony and I are getting together tonight, but he's running out of town for a client meeting this weekend. He doesn't normally work on the weekends, but this is a special case where they are really trying to pull out all the stops for this new client."

Allison pulls out her phone and looks at her calendar.

"I don't have anything planned. I met a new guy but we're still in the honeymoon stage, you know. But no dates this weekend. You wanna have a girl's night? Maybe go out for a couple drinks?" she offers.

"Yes, I'd love to have a girl's night. New guy? You'll have to tell me more. Plus, I have some things I want to run by you."

"Sure thing," Allison exits my office, "I'll just call or text you tomorrow and we'll figure out the details.

"Sounds good."

I glance at my watch. It's 4:30.

The day has gone by fast and I've gotten a ton of work done. I might sneak out of the office a little early and get a manicure before my date with Tony tonight. I could use a little pamper time. Packing up my things, I get ready to leave when Tim surprises me on the way out…again.

Brow raised, "Leaving early today, Talia?"

Caught, red handed!

I start talking, fast, "Well, it's been a crazy couple of weeks, and I've had a chance to catch up on a lot of work today in the office and..."I stammer.

Tim puts his hand up to stop my endless babbling.

"Talia, Talia, it's okay. You have no complaints from me. Anytime you want to leave early or work from home one afternoon, that's okay. You're the boss of your department so I trust you know what's going on and have it handled."

Then, he leans over and whispers in my ear.

"And, soon you'll be the boss of much more than your department when you take me up on my offer."

He winks and walks away confidently. "Have a nice weekend."

I stand there for a moment. He fully expects me to take him up on his offer, and why wouldn't he? Only a fool would turn something like this down. Yet I know in my heart that my decision isn't definite.

❧

I leave the office, get my nails done, then head home to get ready for my date with Tony. I spend some time with Jasmine before Zack picks her up for the weekend. It will be a reprieve for me to spend some alone time, thinking about what I want to do.

"How was your day, baby?"

Excited, as usual, Jasmine goes through all the details of her day, from her fun sparkly art project to details about her new best friend, Elizabeth. My daughter is a social butterfly, so she has a new best friend every week

"What about you, Mommy? How was your day?"

We are in Jasmine's room and she is putting together a puzzle on the floor. I lay down on the floor with her and start working with her on the puzzle.

"Mommy had a pretty good day. I got a lot of work done, and I've been thinking a lot about a big decision I have to make," I confess.

I'm not even sure what makes me share this with my nine-year-old. She is too young to understand the dynamics of what I am dealing with, but it is so heavy on my mind, it just comes out.

She looks up at me with those big, brown eyes that I've always adored. They are just like her father's.

"What kind of decision, Mommy?"

She is naturally inquisitive. I should have known I can't just casually mention something like this without her questioning further. I start fiddling with a puzzle pieces on the floor.

"A decision that could be really great for us, sweetheart. One that could improve our life. We could move into a bigger house, with a pool. And, Mommy could buy you anything you want."

I expect my child to jump up from her puzzle, excited, ready to move into our new house with a pool. But she seems unmoved by my announcement. She just continues working on her puzzle, and without even looking up, replies, "I don't need a new house. I like it here. And, I already have everything I want. I really don't see what is so special about this decision you're talking about."

I guess she told me! I've tried my best to teach her that material things aren't that important, but that's mostly because I haven't always been able to get her everything she wanted. Her reaction surprises me. I'm not sure know how to respond back, especially when I was hoping she would get excited, giving me further validation that I need to accept this offer. Instead, I just feel awkward. I glance at my watch. It's 6:00, and Tony is due to pick me up in half an hour, a perfect excuse to escape.

I lean over and kiss my daughter on the forehead.

"I love you," I say as she continues working on the puzzle. "Mommy has to finish getting ready for my date with Tony tonight. You're going to have so much fun with your daddy this weekend. Make sure to get your things together. He'll be here shortly."

As I am about to close her door and walk across the hall to my bedroom, Jasmine pauses her puzzle play to ask me a question.

"Will it make you happy, Mommy?"

I stop and turn around, stumped by her sudden question.

"Will what make me happy, sweetheart?"

"Your decision that you're talking about, the one that is supposed to get us a new house and everything. Is that what you want?"

"I-I don't know, sweetheart. I guess that's what I'm trying to figure out. I thought those things would make you happy. That's what's important to me."

"I'm happy, Mommy. I don't need those things. But you need to figure out what makes you happy."

With that, she is back to her puzzle again. I walk away, closing her door. Did my child just teach me a lesson? She has more wisdom at nine years old than most of my friends in their 30s. She asks a poignant question that I've been dodging the last couple of weeks as I've been searching for the missing piece. What makes me happy? To be honest, I can't say that my job has ever made me happy; I've just been content. Perhaps that's why I have this strange feeling in the pit of stomach, like I need a change. I hope that the change I need will come in the form of this promotion.

Will this position make me happy? There's no question that it will take care of my family financially. For now, I need to finish getting ready for my date.

Tony and I have a favorite Italian bistro that we like to frequent once a month or so for our date nights. It has become "our place" and is wildly romantic. It's small and quaint but has an adorable Italian musical trio that travels around the restaurant and serenades the patrons. It reminds me of the Disney movie, *Lady and the Tramp*, where they are eating the spaghetti, and have their first dog kiss.

After finishing a great dinner of veal parmigiana and lasagna, Tony and I are enjoying a glass of dessert wine and sharing a plate of tiramisu.

"Have you given any more thought to the partner offer you mentioned to me last night? Did it help to get a good night's sleep?"

It seems obvious that Tony has thought about this.

"I thought a good night's sleep would help, but honestly, it only muddied the water more. Tony, it's a tremendous offer and I feel like I'd be a fool to turn it down, but why am I not excited about it? Shouldn't I be excited? I just feel like there's something more I should be doing, like maybe I'm missing something."

"Well, let's put some things in perspective. Did they send you an offer letter?"

I nod.

"Did you have a chance to review it last night? How much more are they offering you for this position?"

I run my fingers through my hair because the compensation package on this deal is ridiculous.

"Yes, I reviewed it last night. It's $175,000 a year and a lot of perks like the company car service, expense account, etc," I share.

Tony almost falls out of his chair.

"$175,000!" he yells, "Talia, that is a game changer. Whatever hang-ups you are dealing with, you need to suck it up and put them away. You can't turn this down."

"But..." I start.

Tony interrupts me before I can say anything more.

"Talia, that almost doubles your current salary, which is pretty good by the way. You can't ignore that."

"Tony, should I be making this decision just on the money? Isn't there more to it than compensation? What if I really don't want to do this?"

Tony flashes me a patronizing look. I don't like it.

"Really, Talia? I thought you liked your job."

"I do, but this is different. I would not be a creative director anymore. I'd assume much more responsibility, which I don't mind.

I guess if I'm going to run a company, I'm not so sure I want to run this one."

"Talia, how many opportunities in life do you have to run a company anyway? How can you even afford to be picky in this situation? What other company could you possibly run?" He questions.

I'm annoyed now. I don't feel supported; his questions are making me uneasy, and I feel pressured to make a decision I'm unsure about.

"I-I don't know, Tony," I reply, "can we just change the subject? I don't want to talk about this anymore."

Tony gives me an incredulous look before picking up his glass of wine and taking a sip.

"Ok," he acquiesces.

The rest of our night together feels strained. I don't have much to say and I think Tony feels like he's walking on eggshells. As he pulls into the driveway of my town home, he breaks the awkward silence.

"Talia, I'm sorry if it seemed like I was pressuring you about this promotion. It's just that it's...it's a big decision and I thought we decided that we'd be in this together."

I take his hand in mine.

"I want to make these big decisions with you," he confesses.

I do love him.

"And I want to make them with you, too. But, Tony, sometimes you have to throttle back. You got so excited about this opportunity when I told you about it, you practically already made up my mind for me. Trust me, I understand what a tremendous opportunity this is, and what it could mean for our future. But I'm not going to make this decision solely on the money. There are bigger things for me consider."

His tone changes. The salary and status of this position are clouding his thinking.

"Like what?" He's challenging me now.

"Like happiness."

Tony waves off my comment as if it doesn't matter.

"Happiness is relative."

This infuriates me.

"Really? Do you consider it to be relative in our relationship? Because I'll be the first to tell you that I'm not with you just for your dashing good looks or successful career. I'm with you because I love you. You could be a ditch digger for all I care. I love YOU, not your job or your status," I tell him.

Silence.

"Look, I realize that this decision is not just a burden on me now. It's falling on you as well. I've got some things to figure out, and I'm not exactly sure what they are yet. I feel like for the first time in my life, I'm at a crossroads where I can make choices based on what I want in my life, not just what I have to do. That's a big deal to me," I continue.

It's Tony's turn to chime in.

"Sweetheart, I get that, I really do. What I don't get is what this crossroads means? If you don't want to take this promotion as great as it is, what is it that you want to do in its place?" He's trying to understand the reason behind my hesitation, and I wish I had more to tell him.

I lean my head against the headrest, frustrated over my dilemma.

"That's what I have to figure out."

"While you're figuring it out, be careful not to let the best opportunity you ever had just slip through your fingers. I've got an early flight in the morning, so I need to call it a night. I'll give you a call tomorrow."

He gives me a quick peck on the lips, I get out of the car and walk to my front door.

Part of me wonders if he is talking about my promotion or our relationship. The curtness in his tone raises my curiosity.

I walk into an empty, quiet home. Jasmine has already left to spend the weekend with her father. I check my watch.

10:30.

Talk about an early Friday night. I grab a bottle of wine out of the fridge and a glass and walk upstairs to my bedroom. I quickly change into my pajamas and hop in bed, glass in hand. I turn on the television. Maybe I can catch a good Romcom marathon.

I flip through the channels, but my mind is not engaged. I start thinking about my conversation with Tony tonight. Could he have a point? Is this the best offer I will ever receive in my career? I mean, how could I even think about turning down a great offer like this for an unknown entity I have yet to discover?

I guess I cannot fault him for being just a little frustrated with me. If the tables were turned, I might feel the same way. Here I am telling him that I was just offered this amazing opportunity at my job, but I'm not sure if I want to take it. Yet, I can't tell him why or what I would rather do instead. From the outside looking in, that doesn't make sense.

The only person that seems to get me at all in this situation is the one I least expected to understand - Jasmine. Talk about being cut from the same cloth. She doesn't care about how much money I make. She doesn't even want new things. The only question she had for me was, would I be happy? Tony never once asked me that question, and I feel like that is part of his role as my boyfriend, to be concerned with my happiness first. When it comes to his career, he seems to have little regard for happiness. Security is top priority for him in his work, which I guess is exactly why this promotion makes so much sense to him. For me to get through to him, I need to figure out some things for myself. I only have a couple of weeks to make this decision, so I need to hunker down and weigh the pros and cons of accepting this position. If I'm not excited about this job, I have to find out why.

Tomorrow, I will try and sort this out. But, for now, I plan to finish my wine and wind down for the night with a good romcom. Oh, Bridget Jones Diaries is on. I love her!

I turn over in the sheets feeling refreshed. I live for Saturday mornings - such a sense of peace. I glance at my alarm clock next to my bed.

9:30. Wow, I really slept in this morning. Used to the commotion of getting ready for work and getting Jasmine off to school each morning, 6:00 AM is my normal start time. Plus, Jasmine is an early riser, even on the weekends, forcing me awake earlier than I'd like.

So, yes, this morning is a treat. It feels good to be well-rested, waking up when I feel like it. I lay in my bed just a little longer, soaking up the moment.

Total silence. Peace. Serenity.

After soaking in my solitude, I walk downstairs to start my day with a cup of coffee. As the brewer starts doing its thing, I sit at my kitchen bar, hands under my chin, pondering the events of last night and of the past week. I have some major decisions to make, and no matter how I look at it, it isn't going to be easy. Some people are going to like the direction I choose and support me, and some, not so much. My initial feelings tell me that if I choose to accept Tim's offer, I will gain the respect, support and admiration of everyone I know. But my gut screams that if I make this big decision to please everyone else, I might be selling myself out. Is that an acceptable choice? The first thing I need to do, which Tony was prompting me to do last night, is find out what exactly it is that is preventing me from committing in the first place.

Getting up from the bar stool, I rummage through the drawers of my built-in desk in the far corner, where I normally write out my bills. I find an unused legal pad. I grab the pad and a pen and then walk over to the kitchen table, coffee in hand, and sit down.

I **need to weigh the pros and cons** of this offer. What do I love about this offer? I write down on the pad:

PROs:
The compensation is spectacular - check.
The wardrobe service is cool - check.
Who wouldn't like to be driven around in the company town car? - check.
Anything else? I tap the pen on the top of my head, thinking about any other pros I could add to this list. I am tapped out.
Now, on to my list of cons.

CONs:
Why wouldn't I want to do this?
Mmm... I don't know that this job would make me happy - check.
While I may aspire to run a company someday, I don't know that I want to run someone else's company. I'd rather run my own – check.
Moving into this position will take me away from some of the creative, fun things I've come to enjoy in my current job - check.
While I like my job, I feel like something has been missing for some time now, and this new promotion doesn't seem to be filling that void - check.
I'm not excited, shouldn't I be? - check.

Okay, I think I have the cons covered.
I lean back and look over my completed list:
- Great compensation
- It might not make me happy
- Wardrobe service
- I don't want to run someone else's company
- Company town car

- Taking me away from fun and creative things I like
- Something is missing
- I'm not excited

As I look at this list, a few things stand out to me. The first is, my cons outweigh my pros. The second is, everything listed on my list of pros seem superficial and shallow. If I accept this position, it will only be for the money and the perks. That doesn't seem like enough.

Looking at the right-hand side of my list, I fear that if I accept this position, I could end up an empty, hollow shell. Sure, I'll be making great money, but I will lack substance and purpose. Or, is that stuff overrated? Am I over-thinking this? I should probably just accept this job and secure my family's future forever. Perhaps these feelings of doubt will go away once I'm in the job.

Or not! I rip the sheet of paper off the legal pad and set it aside. It is time to make sense of all this. If I choose not to accept this amazing position, what exactly am I supposed to do? I need to make another list. What do I enjoy doing? What is my passion? My mind travels back to Jasmine's baby days. Though she was an unexpected pregnancy at a young age, I was excited to find out that I was having a girl. She became my real-life Barbie doll. Though my funds were limited, I spared no expense in Jasmine's wardrobe. To this day, we enjoy going shopping together and I take pleasure in putting together the trendiest ensembles for both of our closets.

I think of that business class I took in college again. I'd chosen a clothing boutique as my business. What was the name of that boutique? It's been so long. I look down at my blank sheet of paper and realize that I haven't made a list, but I may have uncovered a hidden dream from long ago. I seem to be coming up with more questions than answers, and the newest one is:

SHOULD I OPEN A CLOTHING BOUTIQUE?

I **need to find the flash drive** with this old school project on it, if I still have it. I run upstairs to my office and begin to tear it apart. I need answers and I need them now.

As I search through my things, I find myself daydreaming. I envision my grand opening, the colors on the wall, the designer clothes and shoes on the racks.

I walk into my expansive closet. I've always had an eye for fashion. There are at least 150 pairs of shoes in my closet, and I just gave away twenty pairs a few weeks ago to a local charity. As much as I love fashion, I never saw it as a passion on which to build a career. It was just something I've always loved. Is it worth giving up a high-profile promotion for something so uncertain? I need to do more research and figure out a game plan.

I glance at the folder on my night stand. I walk over, pull out the sheet of paper and look over the offer again. I can't make this decision on my own. I need guidance and counsel. I know where Tony stands on the promotion but if I present both sides equally, we can make an informed decision together. It's time to talk to Allison and get her feedback. She's always been a straight shooter and I value her opinion.

Still searching for my lost flash drive, I decide to try my night stand. I fumble through the drawers, sorting through papers, pens and junk.

Aha!

Found it! I take the flash drive downstairs to my laptop and plug it in, hoping that it will give me the answers I need. As I review the information on the flash drive, memories come flooding back to me. I remember how I felt when I was working on this project, the energy and passion. Those feelings resurface as I scan the detailed business plan I'd devised on this faux business venture. What did I name it? Oh, there is it - Trendyz! Not bad! The goal for the boutique was to provide the trendiest fashion forward looks at an affordable price point. From personal experience, I know what it's like to have Sak's taste on a Target budget.

The goal was to give everybody the opportunity to get in on the cutting edge of the clothing industry even if their purse strings were a little low. As I go through the information on this flash drive, something inside of me lights up again, something I have not felt in a long time.

※

Sipping on my pineapple martini, I soak up the atmosphere of the jazz bar Allison and I like to frequent for our girls' nights.

"It's been so long since I've had some time out, I'd forgotten how nice this place was," she says, swaying to the sound of old school Kenny G.

"Yeah, I love this place."

Taking a more serious stance and leaning forward, Allison gets straight to the point.

"You said you wanted to run something by me. What's up?"

I sit my martini down, hoping she will provide a different perspective than Tony. "I received an offer from Mr. Stevens, a very lucrative one, but I don't know whether I should accept it."

"Well, what kind of offer did you get? Can you disclose it yet?" She questions.

I shake my head.

"I'm not at liberty to give details but let's just say, it's a significant raise in salary with lots of perks and a higher management level in the company."

Allison's eyes widen.

"That sounds great," she says as she sips her wine, "but you said you had a dilemma. What's the dilemma? It sounds a slam dunk."

I sigh.

"I haven't really been happy for quite some time. I could never really put my finger on it but always felt like something was missing. It didn't make sense to me because I've worked really hard to get where I am, and many people would consider me successful."

"You are successful," Allison interrupts. "Hell, you're my boss."

"That's nice and everything, but a part of me has always wanted more," I start.

Allison interrupts again.

"Isn't that what this promotion would give you? More?" Allison crinkles her brow in confusion.

"That's what I thought. What I hoped, but when I got the offer, I wasn't excited, and I should be. Something so great should get me pumped up. Everyone I talk to about it gets excited, but I don't. Something is wrong with that. If I take this job just because it looks good on paper and I don't feel right about it in my gut, wouldn't I be selling myself out?"

Allison twirls her wine in her glass.

"Well, we all sell out a little bit in our careers," she confesses. "I don't know if there is such a thing as real happiness and bliss. If you have a good job that can provide you with some security, that's all that matters, right? Especially for you because you have little Jasmine to think of."

"I do, but I can give her everything she needs now. We're doing very well."

Allison sets her glass down.

"Are you saying that you want to turn the promotion down and stay where you are? Didn't you just say you haven't been happy in a while? How does that decision help you?" Allison shakes her head.

She has a point. I am feeling stagnant. Something must change.

"You're right. That doesn't really help me move forward, but I think might have discovered something that will." My eyes light up.

Allison looks at me expectantly.

"I think I want to open my own clothing boutique."

Silence.

"Well?" I prompt.

Allison keeps drinking her wine until the glass is empty.

"Oh, you're serious," she almost mocks me.

"Well, yes," I say, "I spent some time this morning meditating on what I want and what gets me excited and I remembered this business project I did back in college. I chose to start my own boutique and put considerable effort into it. I remember it was the last..."

Allison cuts me short again.

"Wait...wait, you're telling me that you're willing to give up a significant promotion and raise at the agency over some project you did in college?"

She picks up my martini and inspects it.

"Girl, what is in this drink?"

I shake my head because it sounds a little crazy even to myself as I hear her repeat the words.

"I know this sounds crazy, but it feels right. It's really hard to explain."

Showing some interest, to my surprise, Allison leans forward.

"Try."

I take a long sip of my martini to gather my thoughts.

"Okay, I love it at the agency, I really do. I've worked so hard to get where I am and I' really grateful for that. Lately, I've just felt, I don't know...unfulfilled." I begin.

"Unfulfilled? How? Do you think the promotion could possibly help with that?"

"That's just it," I respond. "I was hoping that the promotion would be an answer to these feelings I've been having. I took some time to really survey my feelings on this new move. I even wrote them down and, Allison, I've got nothing. There is no emotional pull for me to do this. The only good thing I could decipher from doing this was the obvious job perks and the increase in income, and while that's all good, it just isn't enough."

Putting her drink aside, Allison walks over to the chair next to me and puts her arm around me warmly.

"Okay," she says. "We can figure this out. I know this is a good offer from the agency, but you're right, money isn't everything. If you're going to make a big decision like this, make sure it is an informed one. You need to be more prepared. I mean, you just told me that you want to turn down this big promotion because of a project you did back in college, Tal."

"You're right, Allison," I nod in agreement. "I need a well-thought-out plan. The project I did back in college was just a jump start to this whole thing, a realization of what ignited the spark in my life. Okay...here's what I do know. I do want to open a boutique. I mean, do you know anyone who has a better eye for fashion than me?"

Reaching back across the table to grab her now empty glass and clinking with mine, Allison responds, "Here, here, my dear friend. You are a fashion fiend! But you know that there's a lot to opening a boutique. Are you prepared for all that comes with it, the good and the bad?"

I sit and think for a moment, swirling my martini in my hand.

"I realize that this will be an exciting journey for me, full of ups and downs, but yes, I'm prepared to take it. This promotion at the agency is good, but it doesn't offer a sense of adventure. It's the safe choice, and Allison, I don't want to live my whole life taking the safe route. How can you accomplish anything great being safe all the time? It's time to jump out of my comfort zone."

Leaning back in her chair, Allison smiles.

"It sounds like you may have already made up your mind. Just promise me this..."

"What's that?"

She puts her arms around me in a big bear hug.

"Take me with you."

I look at her, laughing.

"Really? I may have gained some clarity, but I still don't know where I'm going. There's still so much to figure out. To come with me would be significant risk. Are you sure it's not just the alcohol talking?" I grin.

"Ha, ha, very funny. No, it's not the alcohol. Seriously, Tal, you are one of my oldest and best friends. I walked that journey with you since high school and I couldn't be prouder of the woman and mother you've become. You're a terrific boss. I really do enjoy working for you will be truly disappointed not to have you on board anymore. Here's what I know about you; when you decide to do something, you commit to it and attack it with all you have. If this is really something you want to do, I know you'll be amazing at it. Not to mention, clothes and fashion are a passion for you so naturally, it really makes sense. Yes, girl, I will follow you anywhere!"

That's why I love my bestie. I fully expected to meet some resistance from her, maybe not as much as with Tony, but some, nonetheless. It feels good to have support from someone I care about. I already know my little munchkin is on board with me.

"That's great, Allison! Your support means so much to me. Now, there's just one person left to convince." I tap my temple.

"Who's that?"

"Tony."

I come home, renewed and excited to take steps toward my new passion. I exhausted my mind before going out with Allison, thinking that she would reject the idea of my dream to open my boutique, much like Tony had. I'm hopeful that things can turn around with Tony. After all, I've never really gone over a plan with him. Heck, I'm still figuring out the plan myself. I know I want to start a boutique, but I don't know where to begin to make that happen. I do know this dream has been lying dormant in my mind for years. It's time to act on it.

Tony sees things in black and white. He will want to have facts, pro and cons laid out when I present him with this. I need to do more research on this venture, to be prepared to discuss a strategy and a plan before I share this with him. If I do this, I think I may be able to gain his support, which I need like oxygen right now.

As I am getting ready to settle in for the night, my cell phone rings beside me. It's Zack. I answer in a panic because it's late.

"Zack, why are you calling me so late? Is Jasmine okay? It's 1:30 in the morning!" I'm out of breath.

There is a silence on the other line that seems to go on forever, so I break it.

"Zack!"

"I'm sorry, Jasmine's fine. Relax. She's sleeping. I didn't mean to bug you," he sighs, "I had a hard time getting to sleep and remember back in the day, you and I used to stay up all night talking about…well, everything. I honestly expected to get your voicemail. I'm surprised you even picked up."

My heart palpitations cease.

"Zack, it's okay. I had a girl's night with Allison, so I got in a little late and was just setting in when you called."

Perking up, Zack responds, "Allison…how's she doing?"

"She's doing good. You know we work at the same agency. Things have been…good." There's a hesitation in my voice.

Zack knows me too well for me to hide anything.

"Good, huh? What's really up, Tal?"

I lean back in bed.

"I guess I could never lie to you, huh?"

"Known you too long. What's up?" He asks again.

Searching for the right words to explain to Zack the decision I'm struggling with, I take a pause.

"It's not exactly a bad thing. It's more of an opportunity really." I try to prepare him for the blow.

"Opportunities are good. That's why you left our small town to live in the big city right?" He sounds optimistic.

"Right...but this is different."

"Different how?" Zack challenges.

"I've been given a wonderful opportunity at my job. It's quite amazing really." I start tracing the patterns on my comforter, hesitant to share my problem.

"If it's so amazing, how come you don't sound excited?"

Zack understands me. Everyone else I've talked to about this goes straight for the opportunity while my enthusiasm about this is just an oversight. But, not with Zack.

"That's the problem, Zack. I'm not that excited about it. Although, I feel like I should be. The perks and the raise in salary are incredible. I feel like only a fool would turn it down. But, deep down, I know it's just not what I want to do long term with my life."

"What is it that you want to do?" Zack asks casually.

Zack is so easy to talk to. Sitting up in bed, the effects of the alcohol earlier wearing off and my enthusiasm returning, I say, "I've been thinking that I would really like to open up my own clothing boutique."

The line goes quiet. Does he think this is a bad idea?

"Tal, I think you'd be really good at that," he finally responds, "And happy."

"Then why did it take you so long to respond?" I fire at him.

He laughs, although there is no smile on my face. This is my dream we are talking about.

"I was just thinking. Back in high school, when we were dating. One evening, we went in town for ice cream and as we passed all the shops downtown, you told me that you were going to own a place like that someday. I just always knew you would."

Leaning my head back, I smile. That was so long ago, even I'd forgotten about that, but he jogged my memory and it warms my heart that he remembers. I also remember how his hair would curl right around his temple. It was so cute. Wait....am I daydreaming about Zack?

"Wow, Zack. That was a long time ago. I can't believe you remembered."

"Tal, don't underestimate me. I know we haven't been together for a long time, but you've always been my best friend. I care about you and want you to have a great life."

I blush. He is a good guy. It's a shame that things never quite worked out for us, but I value our friendship. We understand each other, which has made it easier to raise our little girl.

"You're my best friend, too, Zack. There are not many people I can talk to like this. I appreciate the fact that you always see me for me, and you don't judge. You don't think I'm crazy for wanting to do this?" I need some kind of validation to help me make this big decision.

"Heck no! The way I see it, life's too short to muddle around not being happy. I say, if it feels right, then do it." His answer is natural and genuine.

It feels right, but I still have reservations. It is a big step, a big risk, and honestly, I am scared. What if it doesn't work out? What if I fail? What then?

I look at the clock. It's almost 3:00. Zack and I have been talking for over an hour, and I'm starting to feel it.

"I really should get some rest, since you're bring Jazzy back tomorrow evening. You know I need my beauty rest."

"You and I both know, you never needed any beauty rest, Tal. I'll see you tomorrow. Good night."

I hang up the phone with Zack, and I can't help thinking of how good we were together all those years ago. Zack was the best boyfriend, and easy on the eyes. I always thought he was so handsome, and as we've gotten older, he's really matured into his looks. It's probably why Jasmine is so cute. She looks like her dad.

My God! I'm fantasizing about Zack again. We're friends - just friends. I'm in love with Tony and he's a great guy. And, that's that.

Waking Sunday morning, I feel refreshed. I made a big decision last night about my future and I'm elated, a foreign emotion of late.

Lying in bed, I start to daydream about my new shop and the trendy fashions I will carry, envisioning all my friends shopping there. It's becoming real in my mind. My daydream is interrupted by the buzz of my phone on the nightstand. Still lying down, I reach over blindly and answer.

"Hello?"

"Hello beautiful," a familiar voice answers.

"Za - …Tony?!" The surprise must have clearly shown in my voice. I thought he was on a business trip and didn't expect to hear from him for a couple more days.

"You sound surprised to hear from me?"

"I-I just thought you were out of town and would be busy in meetings, so yes, I guess I am a bit surprised. And, I just woke up. Zack has Jasmine this weekend. You're definitely a pleasant surprise though."

I can see Tony's smile over the line.

"Well, good news! Our deal wrapped up early, so I flew in last night. I really want to see you. Can we have dinner tonight?"

The anxiety is building in the pit of my stomach, knowing I have to tell Tony about my newfound dream. I know I'm excited about it, but I don't know how he'll take it. My stomach is in knots.

"Jazz will be coming back with her dad this evening, so tonight won't be a good night to go out."

Tony is persistent.

"Fine, we don't have to go out. Why don't I come to you? I miss you, and Jazz. I'll bring takeout" he offers.

"Yes, okay. I miss you, too," I respond, caving to his plea.

"Great! I'll see you tonight. I love you."

"I love you, too," I say as I hang up the phone.

The peace and exhilaration I felt when I woke up this morning – gone. Why am I so afraid of telling him? Tony is so career-oriented, and really believes in climbing the corporate ladder. My dream of opening a clothing store is outside his comfort zone and world. Heck, it's outside of my comfort zone, but the thought of it ignites a fire inside of me. If he really loves me, he'll support me, no matter what. Right?

"Mommy," Jazz runs into my arms.

I'm so happy to see my little princess.

"Did you have fun with daddy this weekend?" I run my hands through her long, dark hair.

A big smile appears on her face.

"The best," she grins, "Daddy and I went to the zoo and then we went out for ice cream. Then daddy told me that you're going to open a store with clothes. Does that mean we can go shopping whenever we want?"

I glare at Zack who is standing in the doorway of my townhouse.

I hand Jasmine her bags, "Sweetie, why don't you go to your room and unpack? Tony's bringing us dinner a little later."

"And we can have game night?" she asks, her brown eyes wide as saucers.

"Jazz, you know tonight's not game night," I scold.

Slumping, she sulks slowly up the stairs, "I know, but it still would've been nice. And I better be the first one to shop in your store."

Waiting until Jasmine clears the stairs to her room, I turn to Zack, furious.

"You told Jazz?"

Zack strolls into the kitchen nonchalantly and grabs a water from my fridge, "Yea, so what?" He shrugs.

"So what? Zack, she's nine. She's going to run around telling everyone that her mommy is going open a clothing store. I'm not ready for that."

Turning from the fridge and facing me, unaffected, Zack responds, "Why not? That's free marketing and PR for your business. Your daughter is proud of you. She wants you to be happy. You've already decided you're going to do this, right? Why are you not ready to tell people?"

I get quiet and turn away from Zack. My mind still feels unresolved. I haven't talked to Tony, and the clock is ticking on my deadline with Tim.

"You have made up your mind, right? You are going to do this?" Zack pushes.

"Yea," I'm unsure, I mean – I-I think so."

"You think so?" Zack says, annoyed, "you seemed sure last night. What changed?"

"Nothing's changed. It's just a big decision, a big risk. I'd be walking away from the status quo, this big fancy life that I've worked hard for. Some might think I'm a little crazy. I might even think I'm a little crazy."

Zack grabs me by the shoulders, looking me intently in the eyes.

"Dreams are made up of crazy ideas. People thought the Wright brothers were crazy when they built the first airplane. People literally laughed and spit in the face of Abraham Lincoln but where would our world be without the things he did? Sometimes you have to go against the grain and that's okay."

Wow! Have his eyes always been that green, like the sea when it changes color.

Get with it, Talia!

I back away, surprised. Zack has never spoken to me like this before, not with that kind of passion and conviction. It's oddly a bit of a turn on.

"Zack, where was all of this passion years ago when we were together? If you believe in all these things you're telling me, why aren't you living it yourself? Why are you still working at the power plant?" I challenge him.

Zack walks to my kitchen table, takes a seat and looks at me seriously, "Because it's too late for me. But, you- you have something. You've always had that spark in you and I always knew it. That's why you moved out here to Atlanta and got this fancy job. Look at you now. You're faced with what seems to you like an impossible decision. To me it's easy because I've known you most of my life and I what I know about you is that you're a fighter. When you decide to do something, you fight to the end to win."

Zack gets up from his chair, gives me a hug. We embrace longer than I expect. God, he smells good. (what is happening here?!) He lets go and walks to the door.

"Don't walk away from this."

He bumps into Tony as he walks to the door and gives him a curt nod before heading out.

"I've got Chinese," Tony chimes as he walks through my front door.

It is great to see him. It has only been a couple of days, but it feels like longer. His arms are full of take-out food, but he stops to give me a kiss before sitting the food on the counter.

"I had to see you," he says, "I don't like how we left things. You seemed really torn about your promotion and I think I pushed too hard. And, I sensed there was something you wanted to tell me. I'm sorry. I'm here now."

Those brown eyes lock me in a trance.

"It's okay. I'm glad you're here now."

Before we have a chance to speak another word, Jasmine barrels down the stairs.

"Tony, Tony!" She jumps into his arms.

"Hey kid," he responds, "how are you doing? I hear you got to hang out with your dad this weekend."

"Yes, I did," she lights up, "and it was awesome! We went to the zoo, ate ice cream and mommy's going to open a clothes store. I'm going to get all the clothes I want. For free."

Not aware that she'd opened Pandora's box, Jasmine stands there excitedly as Tony sets her down and runs his fingers through his hair.

"Clothing store?"

I quickly usher Jasmine to the bathroom to wash up for dinner, avoiding eye contact with Tony.

Tony stands in front of me, arms crossed.

"You said earlier that you knew I had something to tell you," I smile sheepishly.

"A clothing store?" Tony quips, "Really? Where is this coming from?"

I take Tony's hand in my own, and softly caress it.

"I know, and I promise that I will fill you in, after dinner. Right now, can we just eat? I'm starving," I attempt to avert his attention.

After stuffing my face with moo shoo and watching Jasmine ravage two egg rolls, it's getting late. Jasmine loves to have Tony tuck her in, so I put away the leftover takeout in the kitchen downstairs while Tony says good night to Jasmine. I get so caught up in my thoughts and cleaning up in the kitchen that I don't even hear Tony walk back in.

"Tell me about this clothing store that Jasmine seems so excited about?" he pulls up a bar stool to the kitchen counter.

"Ok," I reply anxiously.

"You remember our discussion about me not feeling fulfilled anymore at my job, like something was missing?" I remind him.

"Yes."

"I've been trying to figure out how to fill this void or what was supposed to fill it. I've been doing some soul searching and I thought back to my days in college. We did a business project where we were all challenged to start our own businesses. At that time, I decided to start my own clothing boutique. I developed a business plan and executed a successful shop. I remember thinking at the time, I could really do this. But I felt I lacked the resources to execute it and before I knew it, I had an opportunity to start my career at the agency and that took on a life of its own. Now here I am."

Tony is silent, so I keep talking.

"You said this was coming out of nowhere," I continue, "It really hasn't. It's always been there. I lost focus of what I really wanted and now I'm at a crossroads and I need to make a decision on where I want to be."

This breaks the silence on Tony's end.

"Crossroads? You're seriously not thinking of turning down the partnership that your boss just offered you?"

His words exasperate me.

"Have you been listening to anything I'm telling you? The agency is not enough for me anymore because this is what I feel like I was always destined to do."

Tony gets up from his chair, ready to defend his argument.

"I heard exactly what you said, which is why I don't understand that you could even consider turning this offer down." His words confuse me.

"Tony, you're not making sense."

"You said you had a dream to start this clothing boutique but never did because you lacked resources. It seems to me that this new gig could afford you almost unlimited resources. With the support of Mr. Stevens, you could grow this dream big. Heck, maybe even franchise it."

Tony has a point. I've never thought about it from that perspective, but in my experience, promotions always mean more work. If I decide to accept this promotion, I'll be putting my dream on the back burner once again. I don't see where I'll have time to work on building my own legacy. I don't know if the reward is worth the risk.

"I see what you're saying. I just don't know if I can balance both at the same time. Tim wants me to be a partner, which means a lot more responsibility. As creative director, my plate is already full. If I do this, it's next to impossible for me to open my boutique because that will require my full attention." I scratch my head, weighing the options.

"Then, maybe it's worth it for you to wait just a little longer," Tony suggests. "I just think it would be foolish for you to walk away from this. This is a once in a lifetime opportunity that has the ability to fuel the dream you're so excited about."

"At what expense, Tony? I've felt complacent at the agency for a while now. You're telling me to just accept that when I know how to turn it around? For what?"

Tony frames his large hands around my face.

"For your security? For your legacy? This position is not only going to grow your income exponentially, it's going to put you in a position to ally with people that will make your clothing boutique concept even more successful. Look at the big picture, Talia! Give up a little bit now, for a lot later." It almost feels like he's trying to beat some sense into me, but I don't need it.

I step out of his hold.

"What if I don't want to give anything up anymore?" I'm resenting him now.

Tony's gaze turns stern, almost cold.

"I know you're excited about this dream of yours, and I support you. Talia, I'm a practical guy. Be smart about this. You can get what you want but be strategic about it. I love that you always lead with your heart. That is one of the things that drew me to you and one of the qualities I love most about you. At the same time, I think that is what makes us a power couple, because we balance each other out. You taught me how to love and dream. I can help you keep your feet on solid ground. I'm not telling you not to pursue this. Lord knows I want you to be happy. I want you to make smart decisions. Do you understand what I'm saying?"

"Yes," I respond, feeling very emotional.

Tony grabs his coat and starts toward the door.

"I know you have a lot to think about, so I'm going to give you some space to do that but know that I'm here for you if you need anything. I'm not going to tell you what to do, but don't blow this opportunity. See it for what it can do for you. When do you have to get back your boss?"

"I still have a few days to make a decision." The clock is ticking fast.

"Don't make the wrong choice. If you really think about what I said, you don't really have to choose at all. I love you." His gaze lingers on me for a while before he walks away.

"I love you, too," I repeat back at him before he's gone, leaving a boulder on my shoulders that feels too heavy to carry.

The tension between us it high. He didn't even kiss me goodnight. What's that crap about not telling me what to do? That's exactly what he did.

❧

As I roll out of bed and get ready for work, my feet drop to the floor like lead. Tim will be expecting feedback on the offer this week. Problem is, I was so resolute in my decision until I spoke with Tony last night. Is he right? Would I be crazy to give up this incredible offer? Would it help me achieve my dream of opening my boutique?

There are so many questions looming in my head, and I have no answer to any them. I have a few days to get this right. After getting Jasmine off to school, I use my commute to just contemplate my options.

How much will I be giving up if I decide to walk away from this opportunity? Will I regret it forever? It really is a once in a lifetime chance. Most people wait their whole lives to get a chance like this and I honestly feel like it just landed in my lap. I don't even know if I deserve it.

There are certainly people in the office that think they are more deserving. If I decide to walk away, at least there will be plenty of candidates that can step in and take my place. Tim did say he wants me, that he trusts me. That counts for a lot because I consider him my mentor. Could Tony be right? If I accept this position, Tim can teach me the fundamentals of being a business owner. He may even support my dream to open my own boutique and possibly invest.

Wait – is that a pipe dream, or is it real? He likes me, but does he like me enough to invest in me and what I want? He's willing to invest in me to further the agency but that's his baby, his dream. What about mine? Tony said that I would have to give up what I want now for a great outcome later. Honestly, I feel like I've waited too long already. I know I have a great job and make great money. I have worked very hard to reach the level I have with the agency and I'm so grateful for that. Despite that, my feet still feel cumbrous when I step out of my car each day to go into the office. I know what I should be doing; I just want to go for it.

Perhaps it is too hasty. There is still a lot of homework that I need to do to make this dream real, but in my heart, there is no doubt that this is what I want to do. It's funny how Zack reminded me that this was something I'd mentioned when I was in high school. I'd completely forgotten about that. This is a dream that has been buried for a long time. Why should I wait any longer to see it come to life? I have money in savings. I started putting money away as soon as I got my head above water. I have enough to get this thing going and if not, I'm sure there are resources that can help me. People start new businesses every day. Why not me?

I practically float into the office, not even realizing that I pass all my staff and go straight into my office without speaking, like a zombie.

"Uh – hello?" Allison queries as she scurries into my office and shuts the door.

I don't even realize she's there until she clears her throat to capture my attention.

"Oh, hi Allison," I respond, distracted.

"What's up with you?" she takes a seat in front of my desk.

Shuffling through the papers on my desk, I look at her inquisitively. "What do you mean?"

Allison looks bewildered.

"You shuffled in here this morning and went straight into the office without a word to anyone. You never do that. What's up with you?"

Coming to grips with my unfriendly entrance, I apologize.

"I'm sorry, Allison. I just didn't realize. I-I just have a lot of my mind."

Leaning forward on my desk, Allison whispers, "Is this about the clothing store?"

I nod my head.

"Why do you look so stressed? You should be excited. That's a good thing and you get to blow this place."

Forcing a peremptory laugh, I ask Allison, "What, you don't like it here?"

We both have love for our jobs but have no love for its demands on our lives. I think we both want something more.

"You know I like my job --- sometimes," she rolls her eyes.

Then we both started laughing.

"Thanks girl. I really needed that."

"Seriously, Tal, why are you so stressed?"

Wiping the smile from my face, "I'm having doubts."

"Doubts – about what?"

"About whether or not now is the right time to do this. I mean, this offer from Tim, it's very lucrative. It's possible that maybe I can use this opportunity as leverage to do what I want later."

"Later?" Allison dares, "Girl, you better get yours now!"

"You don't think it's a mistake to give up this offer?"

Getting serious, Allison leans in again.

"Sweetheart, I cannot make that decision for you. You have to make it yourself. Yes, it is a lucrative offer and it's hard to walk away from. I've known you for a long time now, since high school, and what I know about you is that you've always gone after what you want. When you told me that you wanted to open this boutique, it really did not come as a surprise to me. You've been fashion forward since high school, and you've always studied the places that we shopped at with an intensity that I always found hard to fathom. This has been simmering in you for a while, Tal. I know what it means to you and I just don't want you to give up on it. If you decide to take this offer with Mr. Stevens, just make sure you're doing it for the right reasons. Don't do it just to be financially comfortable because it will definitely do that for you. Be willing to stand on the ledge and take a risk. Remember, no risk, no reward."

Leaning back in my seat, I admit to myself that Allison's right.

"Wow," I say, "how'd you get so smart?"

Smiling wryly, Allison adds, "I guess it's all these years hanging out with you."

"You make some great points and I can't tell you how much it means to have your support in this decision. Unfortunately, it doesn't make it any easier."

Allison comes over to squish me in a big hug.

"I know you'll make the best decision for you," she says looking me in the eyes, "Don't make this decision for anyone but you – and Jasmine of course. But, no one else. You're entitled to be a bit selfish for once. This is your life and your career. You deserve to be happy. Find out what happiness is to you."

How many women have someone they can count on as a loyal friend like Allison? I treasure her, especially now.

"Thank you, bestie," I say, "You know I love you, right?"

"Of course," Allison walks toward the door. "When do you have to tell the boss man your answer?"

I look down at my desk calendar as the days close in on me.

"I need to give him an update at least by Friday."

"That gives you a few more days to think this over. Take your time and don't let anyone pressure you. You know I'm here if you need me. Love you."

Allison leaves, giving me more time to deliberate. I've weighed the pros and cons but talking to Tony really got my mind spinning. He looked at this from an unfamiliar perspective, not wrong necessarily but different. I need to decide whether this opportunity is big and important enough to merit deferring my dream once again.

※

THURSDAY

6:30. Another long day. My team has been working on a big campaign, leading to longer hours which usually include me taking work home. I start packing up my laptop. The babysitter has already been at my house thirty minutes later than she was supposed to and I keep sending her texts asking for fifteen more minutes. I sense that she is growing impatient.

Dashing out of my office, I'm postponed yet again.

"Talia – can you come into my office please?"

It's Tim. Damn!

Turning around slowly, I make way for Tim's large corner office.

Standing in his doorway, I greet him nervously, "Tim…"

"Please, Talia, have a seat," he motions.

I start to argue, realizing that my babysitter is probably getting more impatient by the minute with my continuous delays, but the look on his face tells me that I will not win that battle, so I sit down obediently.

Leaning back in his leather chair, Tim looks at me without cracking a smile, "I feel as if you've been avoiding me."

"Avoiding you? No-no, not at all. I've-I've just been busy with this campaign and then I have to get home in time to relieve the babysitter for Jasmine which…" I am rambling, and I know it.

Tim knows it too, because he puts his hand in the air to halt my needless gibberish.

"Is there a problem with the offer that I put together for you?"

"No, no, it's a great offer," I respond.

"Then, why haven't I received any feedback from you? No communication. No questions. Talia, I've barely heard more than a 'hi' and 'bye' from you in the last couple of weeks. I just want to know why."

I feel cornered. I want to go invisible. I do not know what to tell this man. This man whom I respect and admire. I am not ready to make this decision yet, but it's staring me in the face with cold, blue eyes.

I look up.

"I-I guess I've just been deep in thought. This is a tremendous opportunity that you've offered me. I just want to make sure I make the right decision."

"Right decision?" Tim looks incredulous. "You said that you looked over the offer and had no questions, right?"

I nod.

"By my standards, this is fine offer, a considerable step up from your position now. The salary is impeccable with profit sharing options that I don't even think I included in your letter. You'd be a full partner in the agency, working alongside me. I'm willing to teach you everything I know because I believe in you and think you would do a fine job running this agency someday. Maybe you don't realize the magnitude of this offer and what I see in you, Talia. I want you to be my successor."

Wow! I knew this was a big offer, but it never actually occurred to me that Mr. Stevens has plans for me to fully take over his agency one day. I'm still not exactly sure what it is that he sees in me that instills so much confidence. If I can gain at least half as much confidence in myself, I can easily tackle my own venture. The problem is, every time I think I've decided what I want to do, another curve ball seems to be thrown. In this very moment, I am afraid of disappointing this man.

"Mr. Stevens … uh Tim, I'm honored. Sometimes I wonder what it is that you see in me and why you would entrust your dream, your baby in my hands. Sir, I don't take that lightly. I think that is why I'm taking so much time to think your offer over. I want to make sure that I'm the right fit for this position, that I feel comfortable with this responsibility. It's more than just the salary and the perks."

"Of course, of course, I know that," Tim responds, "I see so much potential in you and have seen it since you walked through these doors. I trust you and I understand that you want to take time to make sure this feels right for you. It is a big step, but I have faith in you."

Tim gets up, walks over to me and grabs my hands in his.

"I have big plans for this company and where I want it to go. Talia, I need you. You are the key to this company's success."

Great. I'm screwed.

I slump on my bed after a long day. Why did Tim have to lay that guilt trip on me? Truth is, I don't think he realized he was doing it. He has no idea how much I'm grappling with this decision. He just sees this as an opportunity for me that is also going to benefit him and his business, much like Tony's point of view on this whole thing. As hard as this is, I need to end it now. I need to decide; otherwise, I won't be going to sleep tonight. Lying flat on my bed, I take a deep sigh.

"This is my life. What am I going to do?"

Glancing over at the clock next to my bed, I realize that I am running out of time.

11:02 PM

In less than an hour, it will be Friday. I've just been offered the job of a lifetime, while at the same time, realizing my true dream that I buried deep in my heart years ago. What if I buried my dream of opening a clothing boutique for a reason? What if it's just too hard? Sitting up in my bed, I realize how ridiculous that thought is. Of course, it is going to be hard. When is starting a new business ever easy? Taking on partner at the agency isn't going to be a cake walk. It will mean long hours and longer days than I've already been working. It will require my full commitment, which is clearly why it comes with the huge salary and all those perks. There's no way I can start my boutique while working as partner at the same time. That task would be nearly impossible. Both would require all my time and attention. Tony is right. If I decide to move forward with this offer, I will have to defer my dream yet again. Is it worth it or is my time now? If I do decide to move forward with my offer and defer my dream of opening my boutique, how much longer will I have to wait? What is the price that I'll have to pay, and is it really a price or am I conceding my dream for comfort and security?

Ahhh!!! So much to consider. I start pacing the room, mind racing from one thought to another.

12:01. It's officially Friday now. Time is running out.

What do I have to gain by taking my dream head on right now? Smiling, I realize how long this dream has been fermenting in my heart. For one, I know I'll be happy because I'll be pursuing something that I've wanted to do since I was a kid. There is a lot to do. I'll need to connect with designers and distributors. I'll have to figure out profit margins on my merchandise. I'll have to find a space. I'll need a small staff to help run the place. I'll need to develop a business plan to see if I have a shot at getting some funding. Tony may be right yet again. Aligning with Tim and tapping into his connections could make this process easier, but it would require selling my soul for Lord knows how long to get what I really want. No matter what decision I make, there will be a price to pay. If I decide to move forward with opening the boutique, I'll be happy, yes, but I'm sure but the ride may be bumpy. There is a huge learning curve and many questions that I have yet to answer.

1:00 AM

I am still wide awake. I sit down on my bed, feeling a peaceful air fall over me. It is eerily quiet in the house. I know what I am going to do.

❧

WHO EVER SAID MONEY ISN'T EVERYTHING? AT LEAST I'D BE IN CHARGE. AND, WARDROBE SERVICE. HE HAD ME AT HELLO. YES PLEASE! (TURN TO PG 119)

YOU MIGHT GO BROKE, BUT WHAT DID ALLISON SAY,"NO RISK NOW REWARDS." TIME TO TAKE A CHANCE ON YOUR DREAM. (TURN TO THE NEXT PAGE)

I wake up with a pep in my step. I'm going to start my own business! I am sure of it, and it's going to be great! A big step is still ahead of me. I'm telling Tim that I am not going to accept his promotion to partner. I am taking a huge risk in doing this. I may walk out of his office without a job. But, what did Allison say? No risk, no reward.

I fall into my morning routine, but my renewed energy makes today different. I cook breakfast for Jasmine this morning, an upgrade from her cereal.

Jasmine is both excited and surprised to see pancakes and bacon set before her. What can I say? Mama is on a roll!

"Pancakes!" she yells excitedly.

"Yep, pancakes," I say with a big smile.

She starts digging in and then stops for a moment.

"Mommy, you never cook breakfast."

I chuckle.

"Never?"

"Well," she says, thinking hard, "maybe sometimes on the weekend, but not very much."

"Okay Jazz baby. You got me. I don't cook breakfast often, so enjoy it today."

Jazz goes back to eating her breakfast but then her curiosity gets the best of her again.

"Why are you cooking breakfast today?" She asks.

I can't contain my excitement.

"Mommy is finally going to start her clothing store," I say excitedly.

Jasmine finishes her last bite of pancakes, gets up from the table and grabs her book bag.

"M-o-o-m, I already knew that," rolling her eyes, she walks away.

"Way to burst your mommy's bubble," I say under my breath as I clean up the table and usher Jasmine out the door to catch the bus. It's so funny how a kid's mind works. When she heard that I wanted to do this, it was already resolute in her mind that it was happening, while I struggled with my decision for weeks. If only decisions were as simple as they were in kid's mind, life would be so much easier.

I arrive at work, greet my team and go straight to my office. I'm still not sure how to approach Tim with my decision. While I am firm in my decision, I am afraid of its outcome. Will I lose my job over this?

Allison slips into my office for our usual morning chat.

"Hey, can you close the door," I tell her, "I need to talk to you about something."

Allison closes my door and walks over to my desk.

"What's up?"

"I finally made my decision about this promotion."

Allison grabs a chair and sits down.

"I thought you did that already."

"You sound like Jasmine," I say.

"What?"

"I told Jasmine the same thing this morning and she was like, "Mommy, I know that already."

Allison laughs.

"Didn't you tell me that's what you wanted to do when we had drinks a little while ago? You said that opening up your boutique was your passion and what you really wanted to do," Allison reminds me.

"Yes, it is, but I've been tormented between choosing that or this promotion, or even the possibility of balancing both."

"You can do both?" Allison asks. "I know it sounds good in theory and I don't know all of the details, but both endeavors will require all of your time to be successful. Opening your boutique will take all your energy, time and effort. I mean, it's opening a business for goodness sake. And, I'm sure the promotion will come with more responsibility. I don't see how you can do both effectively."

"Yeah, you're right, which is why I've decided to be true to myself and go for the boutique and turn down the promotion."

Relief washes over Alison's face.

"It's about time you came to your senses, girl!"

I roll my eyes.

Allison leans forward and places her elbows on my desk.

"Seriously," she's not blinking, "this is what you should be doing.

It was clear to me when we got together for drinks that night. I'm excited for you."

I feel uncertain.

"Why do I feel so afraid? I don't even know if this will work, if I'll even be successful. Am I even qualified to run a business?"

Allison starts examining her nails.

"How do you know if you don't try? Following your heart is all about taking risks. It's time to put your money where your mouth is."

"What about Tim?" My palms are getting sweaty as I think about talking to him.

"What about him?" Allison lashes back.

"How do you think he is going to take the news that I don't want this partnership? What if he fires me?" I still need my job. Savings only lasts so long.

"Sweetheart, what if he does? It's OK. You are about to embark on a new journey in your life. A journey with lots of twists and turns, but exciting twists and turns because for the first time, you are taking the road less traveled and going after your dreams."

I raise my brow.

"Are you my new sage?"

"Perhaps," she says as she heads toward my door. "I understand your anxiety, I truly do. You have no idea how proud I am of you. You're so brave. I know that this is going to work out for you. Please don't forget your friend as you rise to the top. I meant it when I said take me with you. It wasn't just the wine talking – well, maybe a little bit. But I did mean it. I'd follow you anywhere, Tal. You have vision, and that is rare these days. Love you!"

I blow a kiss and mouth *I love you* back to her before she closes my door and leaves.

After she is gone, my emotions go into a frenzy. My inner voice keeps challenging me, *"What are you doing, Tal? You can't take risks like this. You have a kid."* Then there is another part of me that feels a sense of calm. I've been waiting a long time for this. This dream has been buried in me for so long that I'd nearly forgotten it. I've literally suppressed it by getting caught up in the everyday nuances of life. I was comfortable, making a great salary, working for a great agency, and I now, I am about to disrupt the hell of my comfort zone. It scares me to death. Allison said that was a natural reaction to what I was about to embark on. I think what scares me the most is that I have not even taken the first step toward making this dream real. I haven't written a business plan. I don't have a budget. There are so many things I haven't done, but my back is against the wall.

I picture the ideal situation with Tim. He'd be disappointed but afraid of losing me and will allow me to keep working my job while I work on getting my business off the ground. It will be difficult to work this around my job because it is already demanding, but it will at least give me some breathing room to figure out a plan. Eventually, I'll have to walk away so that I can run the boutique full time. The worst-case scenario that I see in my mind is that Tim will be more angry than disappointed at my turning town his offer and fire me. Either way, I'll have to prepare myself for the outcome, and I must be strong enough to protect my fragile dream throughout this process because this is only the beginning.

6:00 pm – a relatively early night for me, considering the deadlines I've been working on the past couple of weeks. I pack up my laptop and get ready to head out of my office, and Tim meets me at my door.

"Talia, great, you're still here," he says, "do you have a few minutes?"

Tim has been in meetings all day, making it difficult for me to approach him about his offer.

Putting my laptop bag down and sitting back into my chair, I welcome Tim into my office. My heart feels like it's going to beat out of my chest.

"Of course."

I motion for him to take a seat and he complies.

"Wow, it's just been one of those days. I've been in and out of meetings all day, working on getting things transitioned from Bradley's partnership role to our new partner," he gives me a wink.

"Mr. Stevens..uh..Tim – about that…," I respond.

"You've made a decision?" he interrupts.

"Yes, I have."

Leaning forward with a self-assured, smile, "And?"

Hesitating, as I realize that I am about to crush this man, I carefully release my words.

"I-I've decided that as tempting and lucrative as this offer is, it doesn't fit in with my best interests at this time."

Tim considers my response for a moment.

Then he starts laughing, obnoxiously I might add. I feel offended.

When he's gathered his wits, he looks back up at me and notices that I'm not laughing with him.

"I-I'm sorry – you're serious?"

"Why wouldn't I be?"

"Talia, help me make sense of this. No one in their right mind would turn down an offer like this. Do you know how many people I overlooked in this agency to offer you this position? Talented, loyal employees with more tenure and experience than you – but, I chose you – you, Talia. And, you tell me that you can't take my offer because it is not in your best interest? Please enlighten me, Talia. Why wouldn't this be in your best interest?" There's an arrogant smirk on his face while he awaits my answer.

I'm not very prepared to defend my position. I didn't expect a response like this. Is it in my best interest to tell him what I really want to do and why I can't accept this position? What do I have to lose? My job – for one! But, it is possible that I've already put that on the line. He clearly wants me in this partnership role, but I know that it's not the right move for me. I might as well put it all on the line.

"I have some goals – entrepreneurial goals that I'd like to accomplish and taking this new position would further delay those goals."

Tim looks at me sternly.

"What kind of entrepreneurial goals, Talia?"

"I've always wanted to open my own clothing boutique. It has been a dream of mine for a very long time, and well, I'm just tired of putting it on the back burner."

"A clothing boutique?" he contests. "Do you have a business plan?"

"No."

"Do you have money or investors for this new venture?"

"I do have some in savings, yes, but no, I don't have any investors."

Leaning forward, Tim examines me, "What exactly are you doing here, Talia?"

"What do you mean?"

Getting up to now pace the floor, Tim argues his case.

"You've been offered a fantastic opportunity to be my partner here at this agency, something quite frankly, I don't think is to be taken lightly. You could be running your own agency or corporation before you're 40. I'm willing to teach you how to do that. You turn down my offer to tell me that you want to open a clothing boutique, which I guess is a cute idea, but you have not done any research on the matter. You don't have a business plan. Have you even mapped out any projections on the costs and profits that you will make in the first five years?"

"Well – no."

"Have you even talked to other boutique owners to find out from them what it really takes to run this type of business?" He continues to prod.

Feeling attacked, I answer defensively, "No."

Sitting back down in front of me, Tim is perplexed.

"Again, Talia, I ask you, what are you doing?"

What am I doing? All his questions are valid. I have not done my homework, but I'm not planning on quitting, or am I?

"I-I don't know. I hadn't planned on quitting my job. I just didn't want to take on the additional responsibility of partner."

Tim flashes a sarcastic smile.

"You don't plan on quitting," he says, "Today. But you do plan to quit because you've just told me that you have plans to start your own business. So, you're basically telling me that you want to continue working for me until you start your business. Since you're so eager to become an entrepreneur, step into my shoes for a moment, Talia. Your star employee comes to you and tells you that she doesn't want to accept the promotion that you're offering because she plans to leave your company to start her own business, giving you no incentive to continue investing in her as a valued employee. What do you do?"

Is this a trick question? There is no clever way for me to answer this. I'm about to get fired!

I stare at Tim blankly.

"Let me help you out, sweetheart, since running a business is a new venture for you. You let that employee go. I applaud and support anyone who wants to go out and do their own thing, I really do, but I expect a full commitment from my leadership team. These are the people who I'm relying on to buy into my vision and help me build my company, so when one of them tells me that they don't plan on being here much longer because they have other aspirations, how much can I really expect to get out of that person? Their mind is already on what they want to do, which is not work for me."

I am concerned and a bit enraged at the same time. I resort back to formalities, "Mr. Stevens, are you firing me?"

Sitting back down and folding his arms, he looks at me nonchalantly. He holds all the power.

"Talia, that really depends on you."

"How so?"

"I understand that you have a dream and that is great. I'll make you a deal. I'll help you achieve your dream, but I need you to help me with mine first. Maybe it's not what you planned initially, but right now, I need your full concentration on making us the top advertising agency in the U.S. I need a solid partner – in you. If you can do that for me, I will help you get your boutique off the ground, if that's still what you want to do. It's not my favorite business model. I'd much rather mentor you in something else like starting your own graphic design firm because you're a great graphic designer, which is why I made you our creative director. But, if you really want to open a boutique, I have some great contacts that I can connect you with, and I'll work with you to develop the business side of things so that you can make some money. Heck, I may even invest in it."

My curiosity is piqued.

"You've got my attention, Mr. Stevens. You are willing to do all of this in exchange for me accepting the partnership with the agency?" He has to have an angle here.

He smiles.

"I need you to more than accept this offer, my dear. I need your full commitment. I cannot afford you to have one toe in the water on this, while the others are working on your side venture. I cannot move this agency forward with a part-time partner. I need you to be all in."

"Okay – all in for how long? When would I be able to work on my business?"

"As long as it takes," Tim replies smugly.

Feeling frustrated, I fire back.

"Mr. Stevens, you said yourself that I'm one of the best in this agency, despite my more limited experience compared to my peers. You chose me for this partnership for a reason, and I'm more than flattered. All the cards are on the table now. You know what I want, and I know what you want. It is possible that we can each help the other get what they want, but there needs to be defined parameters."

Impressed, Tim shifts his posture.

"Agreed. You make a good point, Talia. I need you, yes, and I do want you to be my partner which is why I asked you. Whether you take this partnership or not, my agency will move forward because that is what I want for it. It is my baby and I won't stop until I see my vision fulfilled. You on the other hand, need me more than I need you. You tell me that you want to open you own clothing boutique, but you don't have a clue what you're doing. You're not prepared to be an entrepreneur. You need to take this partnership position just so you can learn the ins and out of running a real business. I'm doing you a favor by offering you this job. Still, I'll bite. You want a time frame for your commitment. I think that we can accomplish what I need to have done in the next five years. It is possible that it could take longer, but how quickly we reach my expansion objectives is up to you and how much you're willing to pour in. That's why I'm telling you that you must be all in. If you give me everything you've got for the next five years and we're already close to hitting my growth objective that I've mapped out for this year, then I will fulfill my end of the bargain and help you start your boutique."

I can feel the steam coming from my ears as he is talking. I am infuriated yet I feel stuck because there is merit to what he was saying.

Getting up from his chair, Tim walks toward my office door.

"Take some time to chew on that. I've waited long enough for you to decide and now it's time to move on. You have one week."

When I get home, I toss my purse on the kitchen counter in a fit of frustration and anger. I don't see my daughter standing right there observing my childish behavior.

"What's the matter, Mommy?"

I try to shrug off the rush of emotions I am feeling and lean down, hug, and kiss my daughter.

"It's nothing, baby. Mommy just had a crazy day at work. Why don't you go upstairs and get washed up and ready for bed? How do you feel about pizza for dinner tonight?"

Jasmine jumps out of my arms, forgetting her earlier concern. Oh, what I would give to have that child-like innocence back. She doesn't have a care in the world.

"Pizza," she yells as she quickly runs up the stairs.

I pay the sitter then slump down at the kitchen table throwing my head in my hands.

Tim has some nerve. I saw his true colors today. He is only concerned about his own agenda. Then again, I guess that was my objective, too, but I still can't believe his smug reaction. It felt like he was controlling me with his puppet strings, and I didn't like it.

I feel trapped. Either I table my dream to help him reach his or I am out of job. He didn't show one ounce of compassion during our meeting today. How can I align myself with someone like him? I don't know how much faith I can put in his promise to help me start my business. Of course, he has the connections and expertise to do it, but he clearly indicated that it wasn't in his best interest and that he didn't want to do it, but arm twisted, would attempt to anyway. My gut tells me that he will back out and keep me enslaved to his company for eternity. Not that his deal is a bad deal, but I want to move forward with opening my boutique. I am resolute in that decision. I know I don't have all the resources or all the answers right now, but how many new business owners have all the answers when they first decide to pursue their dream? Why did he have to offer me this partnership in the first place? If he'd just left me alone, I could have continued in my position as creative director while working through the details of opening my shop. Now, I'm faced with an ultimatum and neither side of this deal looks good for me. The vibration of my cell phone in my purse breaks my concentration. I run to the kitchen counter to pick it up.

"Hello beautiful."

It is Tony.

"Hey baby," I sound anxious.

"What's wrong?"

I let out a long sigh.

"Just a trying day at work, that's all."

"You want to talk about it?"

"Not over the phone," I answer honestly.

"I'll be over in an hour."

Pizza plus Tony makes my daughter a happy girl. I let him tuck her in at her request while I sit in the living room, pondering my dilemma. Will Tony be sympathetic to my plight? I don't know if he will approve of my decision to turn down the partnership offer. He always thought I should take the offer. Funny thing is, Tim's new proposition is quite similar to what Tony predicted. Regardless, Tony is my boyfriend; we are in a committed relationship, so I need to include in him this decision.

"You look deep in thought," he strolls in the living room to join me on the couch.

I look up at him. "It's because I am."

"Is this about the partnership offer? I know you have been struggling to make a decision on this for a while because you want to open up your own shop."

"It is about the partnership, but not making a decision about it, per say. I did make a decision, and I told my decision to my boss today."

Hanging on my words, Tony prods, "And…"

"And, I told him that I did not want to accept his offer."

"What?" Tony jumps up from the couch with a quickness.

"Why do you look so surprised, Tony? We talked about this."

"Yes, Talia, we did. Do you remember the conversation and what I said?"

"I remember what you said, and what you recommended, but I decided to go against that. I realized that if I'm going to do this, if it's going to happen, I need to go after it now. But I've hit a roadblock and I'm feeling stuck."

"What kind of roadblock?" He presses.

"When I told Tim that I didn't want to accept the partnership, he didn't take it well. He prodded me until I told him why I didn't want to accept it. After scoffing and laughing at my dream, he gave me an ultimatum."

"What kind of ultimatum?" Tony rubs his temples, a bit exasperated.

"He told me that if I accepted his partnership offer, he would be willing to help me open my boutique, connect me with the right people and maybe even invest in it, but that would come at a cost."

"What type of cost?" Tony asks.

"He wants me to commit myself 100% to the agency and reaching his goals for at least the next five years."

Pensive, Tony considers what I just told him.

"That doesn't seem like such a bad cost, especially if he is going to help you launch your business. Wait – you said he gave you an ultimatum. What's the other side of this?"

Leaning back on the couch, I close my eyes and recount the event of this evening.

"Mr. Stevens are you firing me?"

"Well, Talia, that depends on you."

An anxious Tony quickly breaks my train of thought.

"Talia!"

"I-I'm sorry. The other side of the ultimatum is, I'm out of a job. Basically, I accept this partnership, which I really see as indentured servitude, or I'm fired."

"Indentured servitude? Really, Talia?" Tony shoots a look at me, throwing his hands in the air. "This man has offered you a partnership in his business. There is no greater honor than that."

Straightening up my posture, I fire back.

"I understand that, Tony, and I appreciate this offer. I know how great it is which is why I've been agonizing over it for the last couple weeks. The bottom line is, this is not my dream. It's his. It's my time."

Tony circles me in his arms.

"Talia, I get that, but he is just asking five more years. That's not that long, not to mention you'd be an amazing partner. Have you ever taken a moment to stop and think why he chose you over all the other candidates that have more tenure than you? He sees your fire, your entrepreneurial spirit. It shouldn't come as surprise to him really that you want to start your own business."

Slowly pulling back, I face my boyfriend with sadness.

"I used to think that. I used to admire this man so much. That's why I was so blown away when he offered me this partnership. But, today, when I told him my plans, he mocked me. He was smug, callous and downright mean. He wasn't the man that I'd grown to admire over the last three years. How can I even consider working for a man like that? He's distorted the pedestal that I put him on into an ugly mess."

Tony pauses. I can tell that he is choosing his words carefully. I quickly grow impatient.

"Spit it out, Tony," I say, "you obviously agree with him."

Tony rubs my shoulders.

"Sweetheart, I'm always on your side, trust that. I also know Tim is a businessman, a shrewd businessman at that. Think about it – he hasn't gotten where he is by being a pushover. He knows how to get what he wants, even if it makes you feel uncomfortable. You say that he distorted your image of him, but maybe he feels the same about you. You're his prize employee that he just offered the highest honor he could bestow upon you, a piece of his company, a partnership. Maybe to him, you just threw it back in his face."

"That's not what I meant to do," I protest.

"I understand, Talia, but I'm trying to see it from both sides so that I understand fully where you're coming from. Tim is giving you an amazing deal. How much time did he give you to make a decision?"

"One week."

"It's pretty much a done deal, right? You need your job. You can't afford to tell him no even if you wanted to." Tony is trying to make up my mind for me.

I stand up from the couch, my index finger in Tony's chest.

"That is exactly what I have a problem with. I refuse to allow that man to have that much power over me. I still have control over my life."

Tony removes my index finger from his chest.

"Talia, didn't he tell you that if you didn't accept his offer that you did not have a job anymore?"

"Yes."

"Okay, then what do you propose to do if you don't accept this offer?"

Smiling, I respond quickly.

"Start my boutique, of course."

Tony rolls his eyes.

"Talia, you know I love you but as much as you want to do this, what do you know about starting and running a boutique?"

Bothered by Tony's reaction but not really surprised, I hold my ground.

"I know that I don't know everything there is to know about business. If Tim never offered me this stupid partnership, I could keep working as his creative director while I did all my homework to figure out a game plan for my business. Now, I'm forced to go all in."

"No, Talia, not forced. You have a choice."

"Exactly Tony," I say as I began to strut across the living room, "I do have a choice, and I'm not going to let anyone bully me into doing anything. The choice seems obvious to you, but I refuse to let this man back me up against the wall. If I accept this partnership,

I'm going to be miserable for the next five years. Is that worth it to you? Do you want to have a miserable girlfriend?"

"I don't know about a miserable girlfriend," he says as he drops to one knee, "but I do want a happy wife." He pulls a black box out of his pocket and opens it to reveal a beautiful 2.5-carat princess cut diamond ring. It is beautiful. I'm speechless.

"I've been carrying this thing around with me for a couple of months now, trying to find the right moment, the right romantic moment to woo you and tell you how much I love you. All the drama with this partnership deal and my travels has made it difficult to find the right time. I know right now may not seem like the best time to propose. You're upset, but I want to be your rock, the person you can make decisions with. I'm hoping everything we do moving forward will be decisions for our own family. Talia, I love you so much. Will you be my wife?"

Talk about crazy timing. Oh my God! I cannot believe he's proposing right now!

Tears well up in my eyes. I love this man. He's picked me up when I've been down and has always encouraged me to be my best and go after my heart. Until now. Tony has made it very clear where he stands on my decision regarding my shop, and I'm afraid of his reaction when I decide to follow my heart, my gut and start my business.

My heart is divided, between love and my dream. Is this supposed to happen? Can't I have both?

I touch the ring. There is no need to rush this. It is still possible to have both, but I refuse to start a marriage in a divided home. We need to be on the same page. I need him to be my biggest cheerleader, my boulder to hold me up when times are tough.

"Tony, I..."

Sensing my hesitation, Tony gets up off his knees, pulls me close and draws me in for a passionate kiss.

Pulling slightly away, I catch my breath, "I know you love me," he says, "I feel it. Why the hesitation? You don't want to marry me?"

I try to turn away, afraid to revisit the uncomfortable conversation we were having when things felt so perfect in the moment.

Tony will not allow me to walk away. His arms hold me in close, as he wipes the tears that have begun to form at the corners of my eyes.

"What's wrong Talia?"

"Of course, I want to marry you, Tony. You are one of the best things that has ever happened to me, outside the birth of my daughter. You make me happy."

"But…" Tony chimes in, hearing the doubt in my voice.

I take a step back from his embrace. I need space.

"I feel a chasm making its way between us. Ever since I got this job offer at work and decided that it was not what I want to do, I feel like we are on opposite sides."

Rolling his eyes, Tony walks over to my couch and buries his head in his hands.

"First of all, Talia, you haven't decided, remember? Your boss was very gracious to you and has given you another week to let him know you're taking the job."

"That's what I'm talking about, Tony! In your mind, you've already made this decision for me, which quite honestly, I resent because I've already made my decision, too. What happens when we cannot come to terms on this? Can you live with my decision to leave the agency and start fresh with my own business?"

There is a long silence.

I can't stand it any longer.

"Tony?"

Tony lifts his head from his hands.

"Talia, I want to marry you. But, you're right, if we are going to start out on the right foot together, we need to learn how to make decisions together, and respect each other's point of view."

Standing to his feet, he takes my left hand, and slides the diamond on my ring finger.

"The decision is yours, so take some time if you need to, but don't make me wait too long. As for this decision about your job, yes, I do have a strong stand on it. I'm a practical guy so the decision to stay at the agency is logical to me. It's what makes the most sense to get everything you want. That doesn't mean that I cannot understand your side if you decide that you want to walk away. It's totally illogical to me, but at the end of the day, I love you. I support you, so I don't have any intentions of going anywhere. I just ask that you do two things."

"I'm listening."

"First, please don't make this decision without talking to me first. If you're going to give me the honor of becoming your husband, I think I at least deserve to know what you decide to do. After all, it affects our future, for better or worse."

That is fair.

"And number two?" I prompt.

"Two," he says as he walks closer and pulls me into an embrace, "As crazy as it is to me, if you decide that you do, in fact, want to leave the agency and move forward with opening up your boutique, please, please, don't act too rashly without a plan in place. One thing I do know about you, is that you tend to make spontaneous decisions. Spontaneity is good – sometimes. But, in this case, we need a plan. Fair?"

"Fair.".

He pulls me close into another kiss, slow and lingering.

Then, he grabs his jacket and walks to the door.

"I'm going let you get some rest. You have a lot to think about."

Feeling comforted by the way we ended the night, and of Tony's love, I realize that I don't need any more time to give him my decision. I look down at my left hand at the sparkling diamond my future husband has just placed on my hand.

Grabbing Tony by the arm before he leaves, I confess.

"I do have a lot to think about, you're right. None of it has anything to do with whether to accept your proposal of marriage. Of that, I'm very clear. I love you, Tony Ellison, and I would be honored to become your wife."

Tony grins as he lifts me up in the air in excitement before kissing me again.

"You've just made me the happiest man in the world," he says. "I'll sleep sweet dreams tonight knowing that I'll soon have the pleasure of waking up to you every morning."

"I love you," he says again, kissing my hand before he leaves.

Closing the door behind him, my mind is in a haze.

I just got engaged!

I float up the stairs to my bedroom and fall across my bed like a teenage girl.

With all the things that have been going on in my life these past few weeks, a proposal is the last thing I expected. But it is timely. Tony and I have been dating for almost a year now. Jazz loves him and will be thrilled to hear the news.

I gaze at the sparkling rock on my finger. I am going to be Tony's wife.

Things seem to be falling into place…except we still haven't resolved the issue regarding my job offer and the business that I want to start.

Well, I have. Tony clearly hasn't. He is very adamant about me taking this promotion. But – we did make some headway tonight. He seems more willing to accept my point of view if he is involved in the decision, which is fair. If we are going to be husband and wife, we'll have to learn how to make decisions together, which will not be easy for me. Jasmine and I have been on our own for so long; I learned very quickly not to depend on anyone else to get what my daughter and I needed. Meeting Tony has been a game-changer, but it hasn't changed my independent personality. I've been used to making my own decisions and steering my own ship for over ten years, and so far, I think I've done a decent job. It's just that – I clearly know Tony's position on this and I don't see it changing anytime soon. I just have to show him my way which, yes, is very much emotionally driven, but I know in my heart that it is the right way. Tony is just so practical, which in many ways is great, but other than in our relationship, I've never seen him go with gut decisions. Everything is governed by logic. Perhaps, that is what makes us a good team. He's the logical one, and I lead with my heart.

Hustling to make a deadline for one of my top clients, I look up at the clock and realize that I am late again!

It's almost 7:00. I have to call the sitter to ask for extra time again. I hope she won't be too mad.

As I work on finishing up the last details of the project, I sense a shadow hovering by my office door.

I look up to find Tim glaring at me.

I glance down at my desk calendar.

What day is it? I still have more time, don't I?

"My time has run out, hasn't it?"

"Yep," Tim responds resolutely as he closes the gap between us and takes a seat in front of me, awaiting my answer.

I can feel the sweat beads forming on my forehead.

"Talia, the answer isn't difficult. I don't understand why you are dragging this out. My offer to you is generous. Now I've offered to help you launch your business, provided you give me what I need."

I nod my head.

"You're right, Mr. Stevens…umm…Tim. I've been dragging this out, and I apologize for making you wait so long. The decision really isn't difficult. Once you've determined exactly what you want, it becomes quite easy."

"Precisely," he said sitting up with an air of confidence, "why don't we discuss your transition into partner?"

Silence.

Tim's gaze is fierce and unyielding.

"With all due respect, sir, I never said that I accepted your offer."

I think I can literally see the fire burning in his eyes, but he manages to keep his composure.

"What chance do you have of running a successful business on your own without my help? You have no business experience? You have no idea what it takes to start a business!"

"If you really believe that, why did you choose me to become your partner?"

Tim is quick to respond.

"I chose you because you have potential. You're a great creative director with impeccable design sense. What I've always seen in you is vision and ambition. You have all the characteristics that can make a great business owner one day, with the right direction and guidance. As my partner, I can provide you that direction and use you as a tool to drive my business to the top. With my help, there's no limit to what you can accomplish. Without me, you will not make it. Face the music, kid. You need me!"

How dare he? Or, is there some validity to his claims? Do I need him to make it? He is right, I don't have any business experience. I have a keen fashion sense, but that does not make me an automatic business owner. My actions are purely from the heart, which isn't a terrible thing, right? People who go after their dreams and pave the way for dreamers like me don't necessarily have a logical plan in the beginning. I can do this, right?

Wait! Tony – he wanted me to discuss this with him before making a decision. Our schedules have both been so busy this week that we have not had a chance to re-visit this subject. Not since he proposed.

Tim does not care about that, though. He is still sitting there, staring me down, forcing me to make what he thinks is an obvious choice. Problem is, Tony thinks the same thing. I know where he stands on this subject. How much difference will it make for me to discuss this with him? Every time the subject has come up between us, it causes conflict.

"I'm waiting," Tim insists.

TAKE A MINUTE TO CALL TONY. YOU MADE A COMMITMENT TO EACH OTHER TO DISCUSS THESE THINGS AND HE DESERVES TO BE A PART OF THIS DECISION. TURN TO PAGE 144.

YOU'RE AN INDEPENDENT WOMAN, CAPABLE OF MAKING YOUR OWN DECISIONS AND TIM HAS YOU ON THE ROPES. BE BOLD. BE BRAVE. TELL TIM TO GO SHOVE IT AND PACK UP YOUR OFFICE. YOU'VE GOT A BUSINESS TO START. TONY WILL UNDERSTAND.

TURN TO THE NEXT PAGE.

I **sit at my desk**, while my boss looks at me impatiently.

There is an arrogance in his stance that makes my skin crawl. I do not like feeling like I will be at his beck and call for the next five years. I feel nothing but contempt for him now. Even if I didn't have dreams of opening my boutique, one thing was certain, I do not want to stay here any longer.

I stand up at my desk and start gathering my belongings.

"I have a decision for you."

Tim leans in.

"And?"

"I guess this is my formal notice, and since you have no desire to keep me on for two weeks or until you've found a suitable replacement, I assume today is my last day."

Tim's face grows red with anger as I announce my departure.

"You are going to regret this decision, Talia," he says. "Are you sure this is what you want to do? I don't think you're being smart. I'll give you one more chance to make the right choice."

Feeling courageous, I step from behind my desk to challenge my boss face to face.

"Mr. Stevens. I've had plenty of time to think long and hard about this decision. Do I like this agency? Absolutely! You have given me so much and I appreciate your mentorship and belief in me. I've grown so much here, but I've also discovered what I want. I want to put my talents, creativity and love for fashion into my own business. It's time for me to build my own legacy for my family. You're a smart and shrewd businessman so what I'm sure of is that you'll do fine without me, and I'll do even better without you."

Tim is fuming.

I, on the other hand, feel like a weight had just been lifted off me. I feel liberated, free.

"Do you have any boxes? I need to pack my things."

Not responding, Tim just storms out of my office.

"I guess not," I mutter to myself as I start to gather my things.

I look at my clock. It is 8:00.

I bribe Kelly into staying a couple more hours while I sort everything out. Knowing what I know about Tim, being the pompous ass that he is, all key cards and locks will likely be changed by the morning, so I need to gather up my things tonight.

An hour later, I am in my car, boxes in the back seat, feeling free and terrified at the same time.

Did I just quit my job? Turn down the most lucrative job offer that I could ever imagine in my lifetime? Am I crazy? Or, am I on the road to my dreams? Realizing that I need to take a minute before I come off the euphoric high of this decision, I call Allison. As I dial Allison's number, I look down at the diamond ring on my left hand. I haven't even told my best friend that I am engaged yet. Things are happening so fast. And, Tony – how is he going to react to this decision? Knowing he won't be happy, I decide to put off telling him for a little while longer while I try to come to grips with things myself.

"Hello."

"Hey Allison. It's me. Grab a drink with me, please. Like now. I just quit my job."

I'm not sure how she'll react. Even I have to admit, this is a rash decision.

"Woo hoo," she yells, "it's about time. When are we opening this boutique of yours and what's my salary?"

I'm glad she has a sense of humor about this because I am freaking out.

"I'm glad you're so confident, but I'm a wreck right now."

Allison encourages me.

"Tal, I know this must be hard. Yes, let's grab a drink and we'll talk through it."

"Thank you, Allison. I owe you. Let's meet at Brogden's downtown."

After hanging up the phone, I already feel a little better. I need to vent a little bit and it is better to talk to someone I know is on my side before I deal with Tony. Who knows? Maybe he will surprise me and be supportive. I call to briefly check in with my sitter and promise a big tip for her flexibility. Thankfully, she is more than happy to stay and doesn't have any other plans tonight. She's already put Jasmine to bed, so at this point she is just hanging out.

When I walk into Brogden's and see my best friend sitting at the bar, my emotions get the better of me. I'm tearing up when I hug her.

"Wow," she says, "Tal, you ok?"

Wiping the tears aside, I reassure my friend.

"Yea," I say, "this is just heavy. On the one hand, I feel like a big weight has been lifted, but on the other I feel so overwhelmed. I'm excited about opening my shop, but Allison, I don't know what I'm doing. Quitting my job was not part of the plan."

"Well, why did you…." Allison stops mid-sentence as her eyes go straight to my ring finger.

Grabbing my hand, she interrogates, "What the hell is this?"

My cheeks flush. Allison and I have not spent much time together recently, so I haven't been able to fill her in on Tony's proposal.

"Are you engaged?"

I nod my head sheepishly.

"To Tony?"

"Of course," I say, yanking my hand back.

She retaliates by giving me a light punch on my shoulder.

"Why the hell didn't you tell me?"

"I'm so sorry, Allison. I've honestly just been so distracted."

She grabs my hand again.

"That's a beautiful diamond. Tony has good taste. How'd he do it?"

I think back to that night.

"It was interesting actually. We were arguing, about the promotion again. He changed the subject, got down on one knee and told me that he wanted us to be open and honest with each other and make decisions together like this moving forward because what I do affects him and vice versa. Then he told me how much he loved me and proposed."

"Awww, that's so sweet," Allison croons.

"It is," I say as I look at my ring, "but I'm terrified to tell him what happened. He's going to be furious with me."

Allison straightens up and puts on her serious face as she sips on the Cosmo that was just placed in front of her.

"Ok," she says, "I need you to bring me up to speed. Of course,

I know about your plans to open your boutique and support you 100%. What made you quit today? What led to this series of events?"

"You know that I had some reservations about what would happen if Tim found out what I wanted to do. You told me to be prepared either way to move forward with my plans because I can't bank on my plans happening exactly as I hoped. Remember that?"

"Yes, of course."

"You were right," I confirm. "I'd never really planned on telling Tim about my boutique, but we got into a heated discussion one evening after work, the first time I turned down his proposal. He couldn't understand why I'd walk away from such a fantastic opportunity, so with nothing to lose, I felt compelled to tell him my dream. He all but laughed at me. Wait – let me take that back. He actually did laugh at me. Then, he proceeded to interrogate me, under the assumption that I didn't know what I was doing, had no chance of success and proceeded to tell me how much I needed him."

"What a jerk," Allison pipes in.

"Yes, Allison, he totally is. And the truth is, I never realized what a jerk he is until, I told him no. He was under the assumption that I would take this offer because there was nothing better out there for me, which is incredibly insulting. Anyway, he went so far as to offer to help me launch my business and provide me with all of the resources I need and maybe even put up some capital."

"For what cost?" Allison asks skeptically.

"Five years with him as his partner."

"Wow!" Allison almost spits out her drink, "Partner. You said promotion, but I didn't realize he was offering you partner. That is amazing, Tal. That is, if he wasn't such an ass."

"My point exactly," I reply, rolling my eyes. "I forgot that you and I never discussed the details of the offer because Tim wanted me to keep it hush huh until I accepted. But, since I don't work for him anymore, there's no need for me to keep these lips zipped anymore." My liquid courage is already making me feel better. I take a drink of my margarita.

"So, he offered to help you start your boutique?" Allison questions, "Did he put it in writing?"

"Of course not," I sneer, "And honestly Allison, I don't know how much faith I can put in him to follow through. He showed his true colors the first time I told him no. What if I trust him, work for five years and then he decides, no Talia, I need you another five years? I feel like I'd be a slave to his every whim with no guarantees of getting what I want."

"Yeah, for all that, you might as well try and figure this thing out yourself," Allison agrees.

"Right. That's where I am now. Tim backed me in a corner tonight and forced me to decide. I saw this man that I'd grown to admire over the last three years and looked up to as a mentor diminish before my eyes. I realized that I did not want to learn anything more from him. I don't want to be anything like him. The road I'm choosing is harder, but somehow, I'll figure it out. So, I told him no."

"Tal, did he give you an ultimatum, your business or his?"

I lean back in my chair, sipping my drink.

"Essentially, yes. He said, why he would keep me on with his business, knowing that I had plans to start my own? In his eyes, this is bad business." I shrug my shoulders.

"Bastard," Allison hisses.

"Yes. Now, you see why I had to walk away. I might have felt more compelled to stay and try to work this out with him if he weren't such a jerk about everything. All he cares about is himself. He could care less about me or my dreams and what I want to accomplish, so I'm out."

"Smart move."

"I'm so glad you think so because I think Tony is going to see it very differently." Chills run through my spine as I think about breaking the news to Tony.

Sitting her now empty glass on the bar and motioning for a refill, Allison wrinkles her brow.

"I don't understand why you guys are on opposite ends of the spectrum on this. He's your man. He's supposed to support you in things like this."

Allison is preaching to the choir. This is not a new battle with

Tony. It has been a tug of war between us since I first told him what I wanted to do.

"Yes...and to a certain to degree, he is," I explain. "He wants me to be happy, but Tony is a practical man, so he looks at everything logically. To him, logically, it makes sense to take this job because it offers financial stability along with the business support that I need for my own venture. I agree; on paper, it looks good. But, Tony doesn't see the other side. He thinks that I just need to stick it out and deal with it."

"That sucks," Allison frowns.

"Yes, it does. You see my plight? Telling Tony is not going to be a cake walk, no matter how I look at it. My biggest predicament is that when he proposed, he made me promise to include him in this decision, no matter what. And, I didn't. I made the decision and now I must deal with the consequences of telling him. The funny thing is, I think if I'd decided to take the partnership opportunity without calling him first, he would be completely fine with it. But, since I've quit my job, things will be much different."

"When are you going to tell him?"

"I can't drag it out forever. Probably tomorrow since it is already getting late and I've bribed my sitter for long enough. He told me that he had to work late tonight, and I haven't heard from him since this morning. I need time to process this myself before I deal with him hammering me about what I'm going to do next or even worse, asking me to go back to Tim and beg for my job back."

"Oh no, you're not going to do that," Allison stipulates.

"I know. I know, but I do need to think this out. I'm unemployed and I don't have a plan."

Allison links arms with me.

"I was there for you when you came here years ago with your little girl in tow, looking for a fresh start. I'll be here for your now as you look for a fresh start as a business owner. That was a new and exciting time in your life because you took a leap to make a better life for you and your daughter, and sweetheart, look at you, you did it. Now, it's time for you to challenge yourself to the next level. Comfort is not part of growth – remember that. That's why you feel like you do – it's called growing pains. Things will work out. Tony will groan and moan for a little while, but he'll come around. He loves you. What you need to do right now, is go home, get a good night's sleep. Do some heavy thinking and start working on the game plan for your future. I promise you – it will be bright."

"How'd I ever get so lucky to have you as my best friend?" I give her a side hug.

"We've always had each other's backs and that isn't about to change now. Go home and get some rest. Call me tomorrow. We'll figure this out together."

"Thank you, Allie. Love you," I say as I walk out of Brogden's to my car.

"I love you, too," she replies.

Jasmine is snugly tucked into her bed when I get home. I observe my surroundings, proud of the home I've built for me and my daughter. We started from nothing, sleeping on Allison's couch when I first arrived in Atlanta. Suddenly, the reality of my situation hits me like a ton of bricks. What am I doing? I had a secure job with a great income - a rising income and I traded that for something I'm not even sure about.

I start to panic. Am I fooling myself thinking that I can start a clothing business? How am I going to do this on my own? Should I go back to Tim and beg for my job back.?

NO! Stop it, Talia! You knew this was going to be a risk, and it will be worth it in the end. I just need to get a level head so that I can figure out a plan.

I sit down at the kitchen table and start to think seriously about my situation. Things have not turned out exactly as I planned. I didn't plan on quitting my job, but Tim really gave me no choice. It was his plan or nothing at all. I bury my head in my palms. Where do I even start? Maybe I can enlist Allison's help to map out a plan for moving forward. Or Tony.

Tony? I still have to tell him that I left the agency. He really wanted to be involved in this decision, but Tim practically forced me to decide on the spot, and Tony and I haven't seen eye-to-eye on this since the beginning. Hopefully, he will finally start to see things my way and help me build what I believe will be my legacy, something I can pass down to Jasmine when she gets older.

As I think about this, I start to get excited about my dream again. I'm not starting completely from scratch here. I have a little bit of a nest egg saved away and I can talk to some money people about securing some funding to get this business off the ground. I guess the first order of business is to work on building a solid business plan. From what I've learned from other business associates over the years, your business plan is your blueprint. So, that's where I'll need to start.

Right now, I need to get some sleep so that I can figure out how to break this news to Tony tomorrow.

⁂

I wake up, refreshed for the first time in a long time. I roll over and look at my clock.

8:41 AM

"Jasmine!" I yell as I leap out of my bed, realizing that I am her alarm clock every morning.

I run into Jasmine's room to find her sleeping soundly.

It has been a long time since we have had a chance to hang out in the daytime, just the two of us on any day other than the weekend. I decide to close the door and let my daughter sleep in on this weekday morning. I call the school, give them a made-up excuse for her absence, and decide to keep her all to myself today.

While she sleeps in, I take the time to fix my morning coffee and mull over how I plan to start this new business of mine. There is a certain freedom I feel that is new and exciting. For the first time, I am about to do what I've always dreamed. There are still so many unanswered questions and lots of steps to get to my destination.

I grab a pen and paper and start to write down a list of categories in no particular order for my first business plan:

- Summary
- Business concept – what type of clothing would I be offering?
- Merchandising

•Suppliers
•Cost to run the business – budget
•Marketing
•Infrastructure – would I need to rent space or start out online?

These are just a few things I need to evaluate to get this business off the ground and I quickly realize I am in over my head. I will need help to make this real. I am already missing the guidance and expertise Tim would be able to offer in this scenario, but that is no longer an option.

Jasmine runs into the kitchen in a panic.

"Mommy, mommy, I'm late!"

I walk over to my daughter and scoop her up in my arms.

"You're not late, sweetie. I have some time off today, so I decided to let you sleep in and I called the school and told them you were taking the day off today."

Jasmine's brown eyes go wide.

"Really Mommy?"

"Yes sweetheart. What would you like to have for breakfast? Mommy thought she'd make you whatever you want."

Excited to have a free day from school, Jasmine quickly asks for pancakes, then plops in front of the television to watch her favorite cartoons while I cook. I feed Jasmine, then sit down at the kitchen table and stare at my list. I am overwhelmed.

I don't know where to start.

Jasmine trots into the kitchen in her pajamas.

"What's wrong mommy?"

Unaware that concern is written all over my face, I reassure my daughter.

"Hey baby. Mommy's okay. I'm just trying to figure some things out."

Walking over to put her plate in the sink, she says, smiling, "Are you thinking about your new store with all the clothes?"

I pull Jasmine into my lap.

"How'd you get so smart, huh?"

"Does that mean that I can get free clothes anytime I want?" she asks, flashing her snaggle-toothed smile.

"Oh, we'll see," I say. "What do you want to do today? It's just me and you kid."

Jasmine puts on her thinking face which consists of a wrinkled nose and closed eyes.

Then, the light bulb goes off and she looks at me excitedly.

"Can we go to Six Flags?"

"Six Flags?" I ask. It's been a long time since we've been to an amusement park. It sounds fun.

"Yes, yes, mommy, plee-ase!"

It will be a fun distraction and a perfect day for me and Jazz.

"O-Kay."

Jasmine jumps up and down.

"Yeah!!!"

"Go get washed up and get dressed. We've got a full day ahead of us."

"Okay Mommy," she says as she leans over to give me a kiss before running upstairs to her room.

Happy to put a smile on my daughter's face on a school day, I sit back down at the kitchen table and let my mind wander again.

I need to find resources to guide me through this process. I'll pick up some books and do some reading. In the meantime, I need to figure out the basics like, what type of clothing do I want to carry? Do I just want to start out online first and then get a store front or do I want to do everything at once? What is the name going to be? Should I use the name I came up with in class all those years ago, Trendyz? I do like it. Maybe the project I worked on in school can provide me with some guidance on how to do the real thing.

I go upstairs, passing Jasmine's room, as she dances around excitedly getting ready for our fun adventure. It makes my heart smile to see that little girl happy. At the end of the day, she is all that matters.

I walk into my room and open my nightstand. The flash drive is safely tucked away in the corner. I whip out my laptop and load the flash drive. I am surprised to see the level of detail I'd gone through in putting this project together. I had a well-crafted business plan which will be more helpful to me today than I could have ever imagined when I put it together. I will need to work on the figures a bit, but this gives me a great template to start from. After all, if I could do this then, imagine what I can do now with the knowledge and experience I've acquired in the professional world. Being in the advertising industry has taught me a lot about marketing and even the power of bringing your product to market. I feel somewhat confident on the marketing side; it is just all the other things that go into putting this whole thing together that I need to learn.

Today is all about Jasmine. I need a release after all that has happened and there is no better way to do that than to spend time with my little girl.

"This has been the best day ever, Mommy!" Jasmine yells as we walk back into the house after a fun, yet exhausting day at the amusement park.

"I'm so glad you had fun, sweetheart. It's time to get cleaned up and in your PJs because I can't keep you out of school tomorrow, too."

Dejected, Jasmine starts up the stairs.

"O-K.," She drags out.

"And when you're done, I'll order us take out. Maybe cheeseburgers."

"Cheeseburgers!" Jasmine sings up the stairs.

I really need work on improving our meal plan. For now, I just want to get off my feet. Exhausted, I plop on the couch. Today has been so fun, but Jasmine wanted to get on every ride at the park, and being the cool mom that I am, I had to get on every ride with her. What I need is a long, hot bath which I have every intention of indulging in once I get Jasmine off to bed.

As I'm getting ready to order our food, the doorbell rings.

Funny, I'm not expecting anyone.

I walk over to the door, open it, and Tony is standing on the other side, a dozen roses in his hand.

I stand in the doorway, stunned.

"Are you going to let me in?" he prods.

"Of course."

I let Tony in, but I feel frozen because I know an uncomfortable conversation lies ahead of us. Tony is a proactive kind of guy and I have been MIA for 24 hours.

Now, here he is, standing in front of me.

"Hey stranger," he says warmly, giving me a big hug. "I tried calling you a few times today and when I didn't hear back, I got a little worried. I know I don't usually just pop by like this, but I just wanted to make sure you were okay."

I walk away from Tony and pick up my purse that is hanging on the chair by the kitchen table. I reach in, grab my phone and there it is – three missed calls.

"Oh Tony, I'm so sorry. I took some time off today to spend with Jasmine, just the two of us. We took off to Six Flags and had a wonderful mother daughter day. Because I wanted to focus on her all day, I turned my phone on silent and slipped it into my purse. I'd forgotten about it until just now."

Walking into the kitchen and taking a seat at the island bar, Tony relaxes.

"It's okay, sweetheart. I'm just glad the two of you are okay. So, you had a fun day?"

I walk further into the kitchen and take a seat beside Tony.

"Yes, it was an awesome day. It has been a long time since Jasmine and I have spent some one on one time together. I think it is something we both really needed."

Tony searches the room, looking for my daughter.

"Where is she now? Have you tucked her into bed already? I'm sure if you did a full day at the amusement park, she is exhausted."

I shake my head in agreement.

"That she is. I could see it in her face when we got back home. She isn't in bed yet. I sent her upstairs to take a bath and get ready for bed. I was getting ready to order us some takeout before you came. You're welcome to stay and have dinner with us if you'd like."

"I wouldn't want to impose. It sounds like you two have had a perfect mother-daughter day. I don't want to be a third wheel."

I walk over, pull Tony into an affectionate embrace, and tease him with a slow kiss. I am glad to see him; plus, I know I need to tell him about what happened at the job. He needs to hear it from me, and I can't shield him from the truth forever.

"That's nonsense and you know it. We've already had our perfect day. It would be even more perfect if you joined us. You know how much Jasmine loves you. It would be a pleasant surprise for her to come downstairs and find out that you'd be joining us. After all," I gaze at the diamond on my finger, "we will be a family soon."

Right on cue, Jasmine pads down the steps in her pajamas. As soon as she sees Tony, her eyes light up, she runs over, and jumps into his arms almost faster than I can move out of the way.

"Tony!"

"Hello pretty girl," Tony says, picking her up as I move out of their way. "I heard that you had a fun time with your mommy today."

"We had the best time," Jasmine begins, and she rambles on to Tony as they walk together into the living room.

In the meantime, I order cheeseburgers for the three of us. Thank God for DoorDash.

I glance into the living room and Tony and Jasmine are still deep in their conversation – well, at least Jasmine is, demonstrating vividly to Tony all the rides she rode today, even the scary ones. I decide to give them a few minutes while I mull over how I'm going to tell Tony about quitting my job yesterday.

No matter how I look at it, the conversation is not going to be easy. I peer back into the living room. He steals a quick glance away from my rambling daughter and flashes me a loving smile, while mouthing the words, *I love you*. I mouth them right back to him and start to feel an ache in the pit of my stomach. I love this man so much and I'm afraid of disappointing him. I did exactly what he told me not to do, and that was make a rash decision.

Although, I'm not sure how rash it really was. First, of all, Tim didn't give me much choice, outside of involuntary servitude to him for whatever number of years he saw fit. I'm not even sure that I wanted to keep working for him even if I didn't start my own business. He'd shown me that he wasn't someone I really wanted to partner with anyway. Second, it's time to move forward. The fact that I'd finally come to some sort of a resolution wasn't exactly a mystery. I had to make a decision and, in the end, I decided to follow my heart. Tony has to understand that. He will.

Takeout arrives in a few more minutes and Tony has dinner

with us and despite our full mother-daughter day, Jasmine insists that he tuck her in for the night.

A few moments later, Tony descends downstairs, looking perplexed.

"Tony, what's wrong?"

He claims a seat in the kitchen.

"Jazz just said the strangest thing."

"Jazz says a lot of strange things. What did she say this time?" I pose.

"As I was getting ready to turn the light off, she looked at me with a big smile and asked me if I knew that she was going to get a lot of new clothes at her mommy's new store."

He looks at me, begging for an explanation.

A frog is in my throat. Kids – secrets don't exist with them. Not that this is necessarily a secret.

I gather my wits and wave it off flippantly.

"Jasmine and I have talked about my dream to open up my own place a few times. She was excited about it then. I guess she still is."

Tony scratches his head.

"What happened at work?" he asks.

"What do you mean?" I play dumb.

"Didn't you say your boss pretty much gave you an ultimatum? I haven't heard back from you on this. Remember, we said that we were going to talk about things like this?"

I look down at my ring finger where the diamond he'd given me just a few days ago gleams. It seems like that day was so long ago. So much had happened since then.

"Yes, I remember."

He gets up and walks over to me.

"Then, baby, why aren't you talking to me? We're partners now, remember?" he says as he holds my left hand up to display the symbol of our union.

"Yes, I know, sweetie. I do have some things to catch you up on. You might want to have a seat."

Tension rising in his veins, Tony refuses.

"I don't need to have a seat, Tal," he says, "I need you to talk to me."

I gather my courage. Tal, you can do this.

"Ok," I say, "I left the agency."

Get ready for the explosion!

Silence. That is it, just silence. I wait for Tony's reaction. Nothing. I try to read his face.

Stoic.

I touch his arm for a sign of life.

"Tony?"

Still silence.

Maybe he didn't hear me.

"Tony, did you hear what I said."

Finally, he awakens.

"Oh yeah, I heard you," he says, sounding irritated.

"Tony, talk to me please."

Finally facing me head on, he says, "Now you want to talk? Tal, what happened to us talking before you make big decisions like this? Does my opinion mean anything to you at all?"

"Tony…of course it does. It's just that we couldn't agree on this matter, that's all."

Pain colors the lines of Tony's face.

"Tal, we haven't even been engaged for a week. Do you remember what I told you after I put that ring on your finger?" He points to my ring finger.

Tears stain my cheeks. I remember, and now I regret ignoring his simple request to follow my own selfish desire.

"Yes, I remember."

"Did that mean anything to you?" He asks.

Caressing the ring on my finger, vision now blurred from my tears, "Of course it did, Tony. I love you. I want to marry you."

"Do you really, Talia?"

"Tony, how could you ask me that? Yes, yes I do."

Tony takes a moment to gather himself.

"Okay, okay, I'm going to give you some time to explain yourself. Tell me what happened. How did you end up leaving the agency?"

"Well, a lot of this story, you already know. Until recently, I'd been keeping you in the loop on what was happening at the agency. Tim had given me an ultimatum and I had to give him my answer a couple of days ago. Tony, I know you're angry, but I really did think about this. I almost picked up the phone to call you when Tim backed me in the corner and forced me to give him an answer. Then my emotions took over. I was tired of being bullied by this man. Everything that I'd grown to believe and appreciate about this man dissipated in a matter of days. He has shown me how cold and cruel he can really be, and honestly, why would I want to partner with someone I don't even like anymore? To accept this partnership would have been the same as going to prison as far as I'm concerned. I would be trapped. Even if I didn't want to start my own business, and I do, I don't know if I could continue working for a ruthless tyrant like Tim."

Tony's tone softens.

"Why didn't you come to me about any of this? I would've understood, Talia," he explains.

"Would you?" Tony, I'm not so sure. Practical and logical are your middle names. And, I love that about you. I need to be with someone who can reign in the free spirit that I can be at times, to keep me from making rash decisions…"

"Like this one," Tony interrupts.

"See, that's the thing, to you, this was a rash decision. But, to me, I feel like I've been making this decision for weeks. It wasn't on impulse, no matter how much it seemed like it."

"Then, answer this for me, Tal. If you didn't call me before you made this decision, why didn't you call me right after? I feel like you've been ducking me," he demands.

I flash a sheepish grin.

"That's because I have been."

"Why?"

"Because I was afraid of your reaction – of this," I said motioning to the heated discussion we were in the middle of.

"If we're going to have any kind of future together, we've got to learn how to handle things like this, Talia. You can't run away when things get difficult. Yes, I am angry with you right now. I'm not angry because of the decision you made. I'm angry because you made the decision without even considering me in the process."

"Wait, Tony, I never said I didn't consider you. Truth be told, I did. I just never took action on those feelings," I defend.

"Why do you think that is? Because you were afraid?" Tony challenges.

"I didn't call you before I made this decision because if anything, I was afraid that you would talk me out to doing what I know I needed to do. You're proficient at rationalizing why it makes sense to stay with the agency, because on paper it does make a lot of sense. But, how much sense does it really make if I'm miserable?"

Tony walks closer and caresses my face, love and admiration in his eyes.

"Do you think that I want you to be miserable?"

"No."

"Then you need to have more faith in me. You didn't even give me a chance."

"Where do we go from here?" I ask.

Tony steps away.

"I don't know," he says, "I'd be lying if I said I said that we were ready to get married at this stage. I don't think you're ready."

"What?" I say looking back down at the ring on my finger, "how can you say that, Tony? I love you."

"I don't doubt that you love me, Tal. I see that. I just don't know if you are ready to take our relationship to the next level."

I made the decision to finally pursue my dream of opening my own clothing boutique. Shouldn't I be on cloud 9? Here I am standing in my kitchen with my fiancée telling me that he is ready to become my ex-fiancée.

"Okay, Tony, now it's my turn. You say I lack faith in you because I made this decision without fully involving you in it. For that, I'm sorry. I can't help but wonder the same thing about your faith in me. Let's say I did everything like you envisioned and I did call you. What would you have said?"

Tony rubs the back of his neck.

"I don't know. I probably would have told you to keep your job while we tried to figure something out."

"That's why I didn't call you."

"What else do you expect from me, Tal? You know me. You said it yourself. I'm the logical and practical one of the two of us. I think about the repercussions of every decision before I make it. The fact is, you've never owned a business before. This is unchartered territory for you. Why put yourself in a financial bind to make a decision that you're not even sure will work out?"

"There it is," I say, snapping my fingers, "I've been waiting for you to admit it, although I really hoped it wasn't true."

Tears sting in my eyes again.

"What? What have you been waiting for?"

"You don't believe in me."

Tony throws his hands in the air.

"Really?"

"Really, Tony. You need a safety net just in case this dream of mine doesn't work out. I don't think that you ever thought for a second it would."

Tony sighs in exasperation.

"I never said I didn't believe in you. I don't know what it takes to make a clothing store successful. That's not my field of expertise, and quite frankly Tal, it's not yours either. It's just something you want to do. Whether you like Tim or not, he knows business and you had him in your back pocket to help you do this. If you ever had a chance of being successful in this venture, it was with his help."

Wow! Just, wow!

᳇

TONY IS A NATURAL BORN LEADER. HE KNOWS WHAT HE'S TALKING ABOUT. FOLLOW HIM INTO THE SUNSET. TURN TO PAGE 178.

TRUST YOUR GUT. YOU NEED TO SEE THIS THROUGH. EVEN IF YOU FALL ON YOUR FACE, AT LEAST YOU KNOW YOU TRIED.

TURN TO THE NEXT PAGE.

Tears sting my eyes as the realization that Tony doesn't believe in me becomes abundantly clear. I know that he thinks staying at the agency makes more sense practically, but I'm shocked that he would show so little support for my ability to see this through.

"You just think I'm doomed to failure? That I can't make it without Tim's help? Is that it?" I challenge him.

Tony throws up his hands, realizing that he is in for a fight, and he's right.

"Tal, I think you are blowing this way out of proportion. I never said you were doomed to failure."

My heart is about to beat out of my chest. I'm angry, sad, pissed. Whatever emotion there is, I'm feeling it.

"No," I point at him. "as I recall, that is exactly what you said. 'If I had any chance of being successful, it was with Tim's help.' Your words."

Tony is mute, knowing he's been cornered. He can't take back what he's said or the pain of those words.

"You tell me that you are concerned about how we can build a future together if we are not fully honest with each other and communicate about big decisions. What about supporting each other? What about believing in each other? How can I feel confident in our future when you have absolutely no faith in me?"

Tony faces me squarely.

"Tal, I have so much faith in you. Why do you think I put that ring on your finger?" He grabs my hand, caressing the ring, "I would never ask someone to marry me that I don't have faith in. I just don't know how I feel about this venture that you want to go into. I'm not sure it's smart."

I push Tony away.

"Does everything have to make sense to you?"

Tony smirks at my question. It makes my blood boil

"Yes, obviously."

"Tony, I don't know if we will ever see eye to eye on this. You're yin and I'm yang. This doesn't have to make sense to me. I'm following my heart, like I did with you. I don't know how it's all going to come together, and yes; it scares me to death. But it feels right. I know in my heart that this is what I'm supposed to do. I don't know how to convey this to you so that you understand. This is way beyond logic."

Tony sits down at the kitchen table.

"You're right, I don't understand. None of this makes sense to me. I don't know how to support you on this." He buries his head in his hands.

"Where do we go from here?" I ask him.

"I honestly don't know," Tony replies, head still down.

Tears are free flowing now. I'm facing the hardest decision of my life, and my heart is breaking. I peer at the beautiful diamond ring that Tony bought, just for me. It has brought me joy every time I looked at it, but now all I feel is pain. I just don't know how I can build a life with someone who doesn't fully believe in me or my dream.

I slide the ring off my finger while Tony sits at the table with his head down. I walk over, grab one of his hands, and place the ring inside.

Tony lifts his head and looks at the diamond ring inside his hand.

"Tal, what are you doing?"

It's hard to talk now.

"I-I'm ma-king this decision for both of us. I'm thinking that maybe it's better that we cut our losses while we're ahead. I love you, Tony. I really do. I just can't be with someone who doesn't support the path I want to take in life."

Getting up and walking toward me, Tony refuses to accept this.

"Tal, this is ridiculous. We can work through this," he tries to grab my left hand so that he can place the ring back on my finger.

I gently back away.

"Can we?" I ask. "Tony, I'm not so sure. We're going around in circles here, and not getting anywhere. We both just keep coming up empty. We haven't even reached a compromise. I'm emotionally exhausted. You have your view and I have mine. And, just now, you made it abundantly clear that you did not see me succeeding on my own. What do you expect me to do?"

"I was hoping to get through to you somehow. I just don't want to see you fail, Tal. I love you and I want you to succeed. You're the smartest woman I know. Your future is bright. I just want to help you make the right decision, that's all."

I walk over and place my hands over Tony's.

"This is the right decision – for me. I need you to support that decision. Can you do that?"

Tony looks down at the ring sparkling in his hand then back up at me, defeated.

"I'm sorry, Tal. I just can't get behind this."

My heart shatters at his words.

"Okay," I say, "then I guess we have nothing more to talk about."

"That's it?" Tony asks. "Just like that, you're willing to give up all we've built together over this little business idea of yours."

I shake my head. He just doesn't get it.

"Tony, it's more than just a little business idea to me. That's what I've been trying to tell you. This is something that I feel within my core I should be doing. If I don't follow this, I'll regret it for the rest of my life. And, you know what, I might fail. If I do, I'll do it with my head up, knowing that I gave it my all. I know this isn't going to be easy, but I'm ready to roll up my sleeves and dig in. I need a partner that is going to be able to do that too, that is going to be able to support me and lift me up when things get hard. You've just told me that you are not that person. What more is there to say?"

Tony walks to my door, head hung low.

"I guess there isn't anything more to say other than I love you. Isn't that enough?" He asks.

I kiss him, pouring the rainbow of emotions I'm feeling into our kiss. Our last kiss.

"I love you, too," I say, "but no, love isn't enough. I need all the other stuff too. It just won't work."

Tony caresses my face, wiping away my tears, his own eyes starting to glisten

"It's a shame," he says, "we would have been really great together."

He kisses me one last time on my forehead, and then he leaves.

Forever.

I fall into a pitiful heap on my kitchen floor and just cry. I didn't know it would hurt so much. I cry the rest of the night, mourning our relationship. Why can't Tony just see it? I hate that he can't wrap his head around this and just support me. I don't know if my heart can heal from this pain. What about Jasmine? She is going to be devastated when she finds out. She loves Tony almost as much as I do. But it had to be done. I've decided to move forward on this journey, and I need all the support I can get. It never occurred to me that there would be casualties along the way, the first being my relationship with Tony. I wonder what other surprises are waiting around the corner. I knew he wasn't crazy about the idea that I wanted to open my own clothing boutique, but I hoped that he would eventually warm up to the idea and help me figure this thing out. I hate that this ended our relationship; I need him. I need someone to love and hold me when things aren't going like I planned. Who is going to do that now? How am I going to make it through this? I need a friend. I look at the clock.

11:59 PM

I start to dial Allison's number but stop. I call Zack instead. No one understands me like him.

"Hello."

"Z-Zack," my voice sounds cracked and weak.

"Talia, what's wrong? Are you okay?"

I break down all over again.

"No Zack, I'm not okay. I'm a mess."

"Talk to me."

"Tony and I broke up," I confess.

"No," he sounds genuine, "I know how much you cared about him. What happened?"

"He proposed Zack. I was going to marry him. I thought we were going to be happy together," I sob.

"What happened?"

"He doesn't believe in me."

"That doesn't sound right. He loves you. How could he not believe in you?"

"He couldn't get behind my new business venture. Zack, I quit my job."

"What?!" He yells.

"Yeah, we haven't caught up in a bit, although things have been accelerating at a record pace. Here's the short version. I turned down my boss's offer. He was a pompous ass about it, told me that I needed him to advance my career and successfully start my business," I begin.

"He what?!" Zack is incredulous.

"Yes, Tim is a real piece of work. I didn't learn that until I told him know. I'm guessing he's not used to that - people telling him no. He offered to help me start my business if I'd go all in on the partnership for at least 5 years. In theory it seems nice, but I realized I'm done putting my dream on the back burner, so I said no to that, too. Since Tim basically told me I was out of a job if I didn't accept the partnership, I quit."

"Good for you, Talia."

"You think so, because I'm scared out of my mind. I gave up the only stability I have to pursue a dream that's really fragile right now." I wipe the corners of my eyes.

Zack is so calm and doesn't miss a beat.

"Don't worry. I can help you and Jasmine for a while. It's the least I can do, being so far away and all."

"Zack, you already do plenty to support Jasmine."

"I can do more," he adds, "and I want to. Let me do this for you, Talia."

I groan. I hate being vulnerable. I've worked so hard to get on my feet; I hate the idea of needing help now.

"Okay, but we won't need much. I have savings."

"Invest that in your business," Zack commands, "let me help you guys stay on your feet."

I'm stubborn.

"We'll see."

"There you go," he says, "so pigheaded. You hate accepting help from anybody."

"Damn right."

"Wait...what does all of this have to do with Tony and why you guys broke up?" Zack questions.

I'm going to start crying again. The tear streaks just dried. I was happy to have a little distraction these last few minutes.

"Tony wanted me to accept the partnership. He's practical. He sees things in black and white. He had a hard time wrapping his head around my dream to start my boutique. Ultimately, it just ripped us apart."

"I'm sorry to hear that, Talia. You guys seemed really good together."

I'm in my bedroom now, lying back on my bed.

"I thought so, but this was a test to our relationship, and we failed miserably. "

I'm silent on the line for a second.

"What about you Zack?"

"What do you mean?"

"I mean, why are you so supportive? Why don't you think I'm ruining my life and I'm doomed to failure because I quit my job and I'm pursuing this pipe dream."

Zack laughs.

"First of all, it's not a pipe dream. This is real. And, no I don't think you're ruining your life. I think your ambitious and brave, and you're going for it. It's one of the things I've always loved about you, Talia - your tenacity. Nothing is doomed to fail in your hands. When you set your mind to something, it's going to happen. That's how I know your boutique is going to be successful."

I'm in awe of his description of me. Most men don't have that many good things to say about their ex. I didn't realize he still felt that way about me.

"You see all that in me, Zack?"

"I've always seen it in you, Talia. You're amazing, don't you know that?"

I blush, thinking about him. It feels like we're dating again, staying up having our late-night conversations. He is so easy to talk to. I've always been free to be myself around him. I miss that.

"I guess I don't, but it feels good to be reminded. Thank you for that." I look at the clock and see that we've been droning on for an hour.

"I don't want to keep you up any later. Thanks for listening to me."

"Are you going to be okay?" He sounds uneasy.

"Yeah, I'll be fine. I'm gonna call Allison and see if I can bribe her to come over here, just in case I start crying again in the middle of the night, which I'm sure will happen."

"Oh Tal, I wish I could be there with you. You sound like you just need to be held."

That would be nice. Zack's strong arms would be a tremendous comfort to me right now.

"I'd love to be held, but I'll just have to settle for your voice and Allison's comfort. I'm okay, really," I assure him.

"Okay, you'll call me later, though?" he prompts.

"Yes, sir," I promise, "I'll call you later."

"Okay, Tal. Have a good night. Get some rest. I promise, it will get better."

God, I hope so.

"Good night, Zack."

"Sweet dreams, sweetheart."

Sweetheart? He hasn't called me that since…since we were dating back in high school. Could he be…could I…No.

I glance the clock and see that it is now after 1:00 AM. Allison might curse me out, but I need her right now. I dial her number.

"He-llo," a groggy Allison answers.

"I woke you," I say apologetically.

"It's not exactly daylight hours, Tal. What time is it, anyway?"

"It's after one o'clock."

"Geez Tal. What are you doing calling at this hour? Is everything ok?"

"No, Allie, I need you," I feel the tears starting up again.

"What's wrong, Tal?"

"Tony and I broke up."

"I'll be right over," no questions asked.

Allison is here in a few short minutes. Her apartment is just ten minutes away. I remember when I was looking for a new place,

Allison had gone with me on all the showings. Having been in Atlanta much longer than me, she was able to advise of the best areas to live in, and wouldn't you know it, I ended up just ten minutes down the road from her.

I hear a light knock at the front door.

I open it and immediately Allison sees the tears in my eyes and rushes in to hug me.

"What happened?" she asks, concerned.

"Let's go sit down in the living room. Our voices can easily carry upstairs from here and I don't want to wake Jasmine."

Although, things did get heated when Tony was here. I hope she didn't hear anything.

I close the front door and we go into the living room and settle down on the couch.

"What happened with you and Tony?" she asks gently, "You just got engaged. I thought things were going well for you."

"They were, except for one thing."

"What's that?"

"He never fully supported me wanting to go out on my own to start this boutique."

Allison lowers her head in disappointment.

"Aww sweetie," she says apologetically, "I remember you telling me a little bit about this, but I thought he'd come around."

"Me too," I nod, "I understood his struggle with this at first. But, in the end, he just kept pushing me in different direction. He doesn't want me to do this, Allison. Am I wrong for wanting to pursue this?"

Allison is quick to come to my defense.

"Absolutely not. You have a right to pursue your dreams. Don't you dare let him take that away from you."

Tony's words ring in my head, *"If you had any chance of being successful, it was with Tim."*

Allison can see the wheels turning in my head.

"What are you thinking?"

"I was thinking about something Tony said tonight."

"What did he say?"

"He said that if I had any chance of being successful with this business, it was with Tim."

"That bastard!" Allison asserts, "Does he not believe in you at all?"

"See?" I say pointing at Allison because she sees my point exactly, "that's exactly what I told him. He doesn't believe I can do this. He has no faith in me at all. How can I be in a relationship with someone who doesn't believe in me?"

As his word haunt my mind, doubt sets in.

"Or, did he have a point?"

"Tal, you can't seriously think he does?"

I wonder if I'm qualified to do this. Could Tony be right?

"Some of his points were valid, Allison. I don't have any experience doing this. I don't know what I'm doing. I just have a feeling within me that it's what I should be doing, what I want to do with my life."

"That's all you need," Allison reassures me, "Tony can't see it because he doesn't have faith. Faith is knowing that it's going to happen even if you don't know how. Do you have faith, Tal?"

I run my hands through my hair anxiously. I thought I did, but now I don't know.

"I don't know, Allison. I feel like my faith is shaken. It's hard for me to ignore all the things Tony said because as much as I try to say they don't matter; this was the man I was going to marry. His opinion matters to me."

"I get that, Tal. You took a big step tonight, a painful one. As much as you love this man, and I know you do, because you were going to share your life with him, you said no to that because he couldn't latch on to your dream and support you in it. No matter how confused you might feel right now, I know how powerful your dream is because you were willing to give up a meaningful relationship to pursue it."

"You don't think it was a mistake? Breaking up with Tony?" I look at her, doubtful.

"Do you?" Allison challenges back. "You just told me exactly why you broke up with him. Can you build a life with someone who sincerely can't get behind your dream to start this boutique?"

I bury my head between my legs.

"Am I meant to do this? Am I going down the wrong path?" I feel so confused right now.

Allison hugs my shoulders.

"Sweetheart, nothing in life is 100% certain. That's why we must go on faith. I think you've received all the signs you need to go ahead with your dream. You know that you have my full support. I think that you've allowed Tony to get in your head too much and now you're doubting yourself. Do you still think you can do this?"

I lift my head up and look at my friend.

"I honestly don't know," I answer honestly.

"Don't you think you owe it to yourself to try? You've sacrificed a lot to go down this path – your job at the agency and with that your sense of security and now your relationship with Tony. Maybe you need to challenge yourself and see exactly what you're made of."

I start to think about what led me down this path in the first place. When I completed my project in college, I constructed a business model that impressed my professor. Back then, I remember telling myself that I'd make this model real one day. Then, I think back to high school when Zack and I were still together. There was a little boutique in our small home town that I always admired. Every time we passed that place, I said to myself, 'I'm going to have a place like that someday.' Allison is right. Someday is now.

"You're right, Allison. I haven't come this far to turn back now. I've sacrificed a lot, things I never envisioned that I would have to sacrifice to do this. I just hope that it's worth it."

"That's all up to you, Tal," Allison squeezes my hand, "When we sat down that night over drinks and you told me about this, I was genuinely happy for you, and I still am. But, let's not kid ourselves here. You are in for a journey. This is just the beginning. It's not going to be easy. I do think it will be worth it if you decide to stick it out and see it to the finish line."

"Who knows. Maybe Tony will come to his senses and decide to support me," I say hopefully.

"He might," Allison says aloofly, "but even if he doesn't, you need to be okay with that."

We sit in silence for a while. I'm not okay with that. I want Tony back with every fiber of my being. He is the man I love. It is hard to just let him go. I need his support and he isn't giving it to me.

I feel Allison rub her hands on my back.

"You think you're going to be okay?"

"Yea," I heave slowly. "It's just going to take some time. This was a big blow."

"I can sleep on the couch tonight in case you need me," she offers.

"You don't have to sleep on the couch. I have a guest room, remember?"

"Oh good," Allison says, "because I really didn't want to sleep on the couch. Okay, I'll stay tonight in case you need me. You need a friend tonight."

I give Allison a long hug. I don't know what I'd do without her.

"Now, let's go to bed," she says.

We head up the stairs; she goes into the guest room and I head to my room. I'm not sure how much sleep I am going to get tonight. My mind won't shut off. I want to pursue this dream, open my boutique; I just always thought Tony would be by my side as I start this journey. I need him so much. Why can't he just believe in me? The tears start streaming down my face again as I lay in my bed. This hurts. I lean over and find some sleeping pills in my nightstand. I grab a quick glass of water and take the pills. I need some relief from the ache in my heart. I try to turn my thoughts off, even if for just a few hours. I lay in bed and sleep eventually drifts over me.

I awake feeling refreshed. Then, then the memories of last night rush my mind like a flood. It wasn't a dream. Tony and I are done. I peer over at my bedside clock.

10:00 AM

"Jasmine!" I yell, leaping from the bed, afraid of getting admonished for a late child at school after just pulling her from school the previous day.

I look in her room. No Jasmine.

I come rushing down the stairs.

"Jasmine?!"

"She's at school," Allison is looking her phone, fresh cup of coffee in her hand.

"Would you like a cup?" she waves her cup at me. "You look like you could use one."

"Yes, please."

Allison walks over to the coffee pot and pours me a cup as I sit down on one of the bar stools and slump over the counter.

"Thank you for getting her ready," I blow on the piping hot cup of coffee.

"I love your daughter, my God-daughter. I got up early this morning anyway to go home and get some fresh clothes and shower. I saw how good you were sleeping, so I thought I would come back and make sure Jasmine got off to school in case you were not up yet."

"Thank you," I say, then look at the clock again, "but, don't you have to be at work?"

Allison is dressed, but not in work clothes. She's wearing jeans and a nice paisley sleeveless blouse.

"No, I called in a sick day today," she grins devilishly.

"You don't look sick to me," I say sarcastically.

"My friend needed me," her compassionate eyes hold mine, "so here I am."

"You know I love you, right? You didn't have to take a day off. I'm think I'm okay. I just need to figure out my life."

"That's why I'm here," Allison says excitedly, "I thought we could do some market research today."

"Market research?"

"Yes," she says, "you want to open a clothing boutique, so I made a list of some local boutiques that we can visit today to learn first-hand how we want to set up yours."

"Really?" My eyes dance with excitement.

"Really," she says, "now get showered and dressed. We've got a lot of places to visit."

I get up, giddy. Without Allison's help, I don't know what I would do. She helps keep the flame lit so that I realize what is important.

I start walking up the steps to my bedroom and briefly stop short.

"Allie, thank you."

She smiles warmly.

"Of course. Go get dressed," she orders.

Allison and I have a good day. We go downtown to several different boutiques and begin our market research. We go to clothing boutiques, shoe and accessory boutiques, and even a few consignment shops. It is liberating and fun to go out and do something that is moving me forward with my own vision for my life, even if some people have chosen not to go down this path with me. After being out for a few hours, Allison and I stop and grab lunch in a quaint downtown cafe.

"Did you have a favorite place that we visited today?" she asks.

I reflect on all the places we visited.

"You know they all were great and very different. Each had their own personality and flair, but that accessory place was cute. I liked their setup. What was the name?"

"I think it was something like Funky Trinkets." Allison is looking down at a small notepad with her notes from the day, "Yep, that was the name, Funky Trinkets."

The server brings our drinks and we each take a refreshing sip.

"I know you enjoyed going out to these places today and they were a terrific distraction from the Tony fiasco. But, have you given any thought to the type of boutique you want to open? Do you want to do clothing, accessories or both?"

"That's a good question," I reply, thinking hard about what I want. "I'm not exactly sure. I love both but, I also know accessories can make a dull outfit pop. I'm also thinking that it might be less expensive to start with accessories instead of a full-blown clothing store. What do you think?"

By this time, our sandwiches have arrived, and Allison takes a big bite of her lunch before answering my question.

"You make a great point. Starting small is a smart. You want to limit your expenses during the startup phase. As your shop starts to make money, you can always expand your selections."

"What about my online presence?" I question. "When we start talking about the expenses of the businesses, I know that it would be considerably less expensive to start out online. It's much less overhead."

"That's true," Allison replies, "but is that what you want?"

I really want my own store.

"I have always envisioned a storefront. Going out to these places today just crystallized that even more for me. I also want to make solid business decisions. I don't want to do anything hasty that could compromise the longevity of my business."

"Then it sounds to me like we need to run some numbers," Allison says.

"That's why I needed Tony's help. He would have been great at breaking the numbers down for me. I'm more the creative, idea type but numbers are not my strength."

Just saying his name re-opens fresh wounds from last night. I look down at my ringless left hand. It feels bare.

Allison squeezes my hand reassuringly.

"Sweetheart, it's going to take time," she says, "You loved him. That doesn't just go away."

I draw my hand back to wipe the tears that have started forming in the corners of my eyes.

"Yeah, but it would be so much easier if it did."

"Getting back to the numbers for your business, I know a guy that might be able to help us run some numbers," Allison changes the subject. "You don't have to do this all by yourself. I told you that I have your back and I mean that."

I hug my friend.

"I don't know how many times I've said this already but thank you."

"That's what friends are for, right? I'll give him a call tomorrow and we can start working up numbers on your start-up costs because no matter how you plan on getting started, you're going to need capital. You said you had some money saved up, right?"

"Yes, a little," I say.

"What's a little?"

"Around $20,000. It's my emergency savings."

"Okay," Allison says, clearly running some numbers in her head, "we may need to get a loan."

"You don't think that's enough to get us started?" I'm a little surprised. I was hoping this money would help a little bit.

"It's not that, honey. I do think that's a good start, but remember, you don't have a job anymore. You have a child, a car and a mortgage. You need the money in that account to survive until your business starts making money or you get another job. Have you thought about that?" She inquires.

I remember my conversation with Zack last night.

"Zack said he'd help me out with expenses until I get this business off the ground," I share.

"Zack?" Allison queries.

"Yes."

"Are you and Zack…"

"No, of course not," I stop her assumption, "Tony and I just broke up for God sakes. Zack has been supportive of me since I decided to make this change. We talked last night, and he offered to help, but I don't want to depend on him completely, so I'm thinking I still need to find a job."

"Let's look at the numbers first. I want to make sure you're putting your energy into the right activities. I'm going to call my money guy tomorrow. Once we know those numbers, I'm going to need you to put together a business plan, which means you will have to make some solid decisions, like whether you want your boutique to be online only or brick and mortar and whether you want to carry full fashion wear or just accessories. All this needs to be in your plan. Once we have that put together, you will need to go to the bank and ask for a business loan. If we get you approved for the amount we work up in your plan, then you might not have to worry about getting a job because between the loan and your emergency fund, you should be okay until the business starts making money."

"Allison, I don't know what I'd do without you."

I look at my watch.

"It's almost time for Jasmine to get home. I need to jet," I tell her.

"Are you going to tell her about Tony?" Allison asks.

I shake my head.

"Not yet. It's still too fresh for me. I still need time to process everything. Plus, I don't want to turn into a heap of tears while I'm telling her."

"That's probably a good thing then."

I go home and greet Jasmine as she gets off the bus. We hang out for a little while and she tells me about her day before I send her into the den to work on her homework. I have some homework of my own to do. I am thankful that Allison is willing to help me map things out, but I need to sort some things out in my own head and figure out how this business is going to form up. While Jasmine works in the den, I grab a sheet of paper and sit down at the kitchen table and start writing down my thoughts.

What kind of boutique do I want to open?

Do I want a full-service store with clothes, accessories, the whole she-bang?

Or do I want to start out with an accessories store?

What about online? Do I want to start out online or do I want a physical store?

I lean forward with the pencil on my temple, thinking seriously about these questions. I'll need to run numbers on each of these options, but it doesn't take a rocket scientist to figure out that it will cost me more money to merchandise full clothing lines and accessories versus just one of these options. To save time, perhaps, I need to make a decision about this now so that when I meet Allison's friend, we can just run the numbers and make it work.

Mmm...well, I love every bit of fashion from head to toe, but maybe I will start out with a store that stocks just accessories. After all, accessories include everything from jewelry, hats, scarves, belts and shoes. With all these options, I realize that I might even have to narrow this down to start.

What about taking it online? Clearly, I need an online presence. No business today can survive without that, but I really want a physical presence, too. Something magical happens when you try on a new pair of shoes. I want to give my customers an experience. There is a cost in acquiring space which can get expensive. I'll have to weigh these options with Allison's money guy when we meet. What do I have so far?

- Accessories boutique
- Physical location
- No clothing stocked

No clothing stocked…but, that doesn't mean I can't sell clothing. I got it! I can sell clothing online and then give my customers an opportunity to accessorize their new outfits in the store. That just might work! A big smile creeps across my face for the first time in a couple of days. My dream is coming together!

I just need to make it real.

I cook dinner for me and Jazz and put her to bed. I'm glad that she doesn't hit me with any questions about Tony. I'm just not ready to answer them right now. Though I am in a happy place right now, our breakup is still too painful to talk about.

As I snuggle into my bed and watch *Lifetime*, my cell phone buzzes on my nightstand.

I hesitate, thinking that it might be Tony calling. What if he wants to get back together? What if he wants to apologize for what he said last night? My heart smiles a little at this fantasy and I lean over and pick up the phone in anticipation without even looking at the caller ID.

"Hey you," I say.

"Hey yourself," a voice that is not Tony's fires back at me, with a southern twang.

I remove the phone from my ear and look at the caller ID.

"Oh, hey Zack," I say.

"Well, don't sound so disappointed – dang."

"I'm sorry," I say, feeling a little sour, "I-I just thought you were…"

"Tony" he fills in.

"Yes."

"I just wanted to call and check on you. You were so broken up last night."

"Yea, yea I'm fine," I say, "today was better. Allison stayed with me last night, and we visited some boutiques today and did a little market research."

"Market research, eh?"

"Yes, "I explain, "we went to different boutiques so I could note what I liked and disliked about each to help me visualize my own."

I yawn loudly.

I look at my alarm clock. It is only 9:05 pm.

"I always thought you were a night owl. Did I wake you?" He asks.

"No," I say. But I'm more tired than usual. I think it's the emotional baggage I'm feeling from my breakup with Tony.

"I've got some time off at the job in a couple of weeks and thought I would come back down to Atlanta to spend some time with my girl. I just wanted to check in with you to make sure you didn't have anything planned and see if I could have her for a couple of days."

"Wh-what? Oh yea, sure," my mind is all over the place these days.

"Tal?"

My heart is like an open wound. Every time I think of Tony or hear his name, I have a hard time keeping it together.

"I'm sorry, Zack. This is just so hard. It hasn't even been 24 hours and I miss Tony so much. It hurts," I cry.

"I wish I was there with you, sweetheart. I can tell this is tearing you apart. You loved the guy. It will take some time for the hurt to heal. Tell me what to do, and I'll do it."

Why did I let this one go? I wish he was here, too.

"Thank you, Zack. It means a lot to me that you care," I say, wiping my tears.

"Tal, you know I'll always care about you. I just want you to be happy," Zack says compassionately.

"I know. I know, Zack. I just need to figure this thing out. There's a lot of moving parts with this business and I'm don't know what I'm doing. Maybe Tony was right."

"I don't accept that, Tal. You listen me. You are more than capable. You are the smartest woman I know, and brave, too. Braver than me. After you had Jazz, we both were young and scared. You had the courage to get up and move away from this place to make a better life for you and our daughter. I was too afraid to make that leap with you. I've never handled change well and the shock of becoming a father was enough without uprooting myself and moving to a new city. But, look at you – you did it! You built a great life for you and Jazz. Don't ever underestimate yourself. You can and will make this idea work."

Tony's pep talk energizes me and helps me to stop feeling sorry for myself. Why couldn't Tony be more like him?

"I'd hug you if you were here right now, Zack. Thank you!"

"Hey, what are friends for? I just don't want you to give up. You deserve it, Tal. I meant it when I said, I'd help you out while you get started. Let me do this for you," he offers.

I've always been stubborn about accepting help from other people, but Zack's offer is coming from a place of love. I can tell.

"Okay," I accept. "Thanks Zack."

"Anytime. I'll be in touch to let you know when I'll be in town."

"Sounds good."

I hang up the phone, feeling much better. Zack always knows how to make me feel better. Why did we ever break up? Oh, yeah – our lives were moving in different directions. He has always remained a great father to Jasmine, despite the miles between us. And, we have been able to maintain a great friendship.

Until now, I did not realize how much I treasured him. Memories of our past invade my mind. We were happy, young, but happy. Zack always put my needs first, and he was a great kisser. As much as I loved kissing Tony, I think about the last time Zack and I kissed. It was a LONG time ago, but the memory is seared into my mind. His lips were so soft and tender. He liked to tease me, with tender kisses on my neck, then my collar, bone, then... Wait! Am I fantasizing about Zack?

We are friends. Friends. I can't do this right now. I need to focus on getting my business started. I have work to do. And, it starts with meeting with Allison and her money guy to map out how to get this business started.

Allison and I meet in a cafe downtown. Her money guy, Harry Rinks, accompanies her. Dressed in all black from head to toe, crisp white shirt, black tie and studious glasses, he fits the stereotype of his profession. Harry is an accountant, his specialty - small businesses.

I walk up to our table and order a coffee.

"Good morning, Harry. I'm Talia," I say, extending my hand.

Harry peers up from his glasses, a small mound of paperwork and a calculator already positioned in front of him.

Upon first approach, I feel a little intimidated by Harry. He quickly dispels those feelings with a warm smile.

"Good morning, Talia," he says, rejecting my hand, he stands and embraces me, "Allison has told me a lot about you. I'm looking forward to learning more about your business."

I take a seat beside my friend.

"So," I say, "how do you two know each other?"

They both glance at each other posing the question of who should answer first.

"I met Harry at the gym a couple years ago," she says. "We ran into each other in the juice bar and just hit it off. He's an accountant so he's kind of a yin to my yang. We've been friends for a while but recently, we just started dating."

Shocked, I flash my friend a big smile that immediately turns into slight disappointment.

"Wait a minute! How recent? Why didn't you tell me?"

"Now, hold on a sec," Allison defends herself, "I mentioned that I went out with someone one of the last times we caught up, but you've been a little preoccupied lately."

"Allison, you're my friend. I'll always want to know what's happening with you, no matter what I have going on."

"Of course, I knew you'd be happy for me," Allison says, "but you just broke up with Tony," she frowns, "The timing just wasn't right. I'm sorry."

I wrap my arms around Allison in a tight hug. I hate that my mess of a life has prevented her from sharing her happy news.

"Don't apologize," I say, "If it hadn't been for all my drama, you would have told me sooner."

"No," Allison squeezes my hand, "You don't need to apologize for anything. I should have told you. You need some good news." She smiles.

Harry clears his throat indicating to us that we've had enough girl talk and that it is time to get down to business.

"Talia, do you have a business plan?"

"Uh…no," I say bashfully.

Harry lowers his glasses to the ridge of his nose and peers at me over them.

"If you expect any banks to take you seriously, you need a business plan. What did you hope to accomplish in our meeting today?"

Damn, he's straight to the point.

I glance back and forth between him and Allison.

Allison gives me a bit of an apologetic look.

"Look," I confess, "I've never owned a business before. This is unfamiliar territory for me. I'm learning everything as I go. Right now, everything is conceptual and I'm working hard to develop it into more than just an idea. When Allison and I were having lunch together the other day, she suggested that I start to work up some figures to see what makes the most sense. She suggested that we meet with you to do that so that I can start to pull together a business plan."

"I'm sorry, Tal," Allison pipes in, "I didn't exactly give Harry all the details of our conversation. I just told him that my best friend wants to open up a boutique store and needed some help putting figures together."

"Oh okay," I nod.

In the meantime, Harry still has not cracked a smile, but he does open his notebook and calculator.

"Now that I have a clear idea of where we are in the process, let's talk a little bit about this boutique you are putting together," he removes his pen from his pocket.

"What kind of merchandise will you be carrying?"

I hesitate. Wait! I know the answer to this one. I pull out my notebook from the other day.

"Well," I say further pondering his question, "that was something Allison and I discussed at length during our lunch the other day. I was trying to decide if I want to start out carrying accessories or if I'd like to be a full-service clothing boutique. I gave this some additional thought afterward. I love clothes and accessories. I'd love to start an online store with different clothing lines, and then offer accessories in the shop to style and complete the look."

Allison's eyes go wide. "That's genius, Tal!"

Harry looks up from his notepad.

Harry takes off his glasses and scratches his head.

"I don't have any expertise in fashion. But I like your strategy. If the clothing for your online store can be on-demand, meaning you wouldn't need to stock anything, you'd significantly cut costs. Have you begun to line up distributors to stock your inventory?"

I shake my head.

"No, I need to do some research on that."

He writes some notes on his pad.

"You'll want to do that before approaching the bank for a loan. You need your I's dotted and T's crossed."

There's so much I don't know. I feel like I'm in over my head.

"I don't even know what to go to the bank to ask for at this point. That's why I'm sitting down with you. I just need some help getting this all together."

Harry stops writing his notes.

"Talia, have you ever thought of hiring a business coach?" He asks.

"No. Do you think that would help me?"

"I do," his serious demeanor finally cracks a smile. "You seem to have all of the raw materials and creative energy for this business and every entrepreneur needs that, but a business coach can help you organize your ideas into something tangible. I'll be able to help you with some things today, but I think a business coach would make more sense for you at this stage to accomplish what you want. I have someone I could recommend if you like."

"Yes please."

"Great," he makes another note in his pad, "now let's get back to our conversation. You said that you would like to stock accessories in your store. What would that include?"

Now I am in my zone.

"Belts, scarves and shoes mostly," I say. "And maybe even jewelry. I guess that will depend on the distributors that I partner with to merchandise the store."

"Are you looking at building a brick-and-mortar store, or just online? That will make a dramatic difference in funding."

"Yes, I know it does. I want a physical store. I want my customers to come in and try things on and see how they look on them, and I'll help style them. Of course, I want a website as well because no business can survive without a website, but I want my business to have a physical address."

Harry takes off his glasses and crinkles his brow. I feel like he's about to drop a bomb on me.

"What?"

"Okay, Talia, let's get serious here. This venture of yours is looking expensive."

"How expensive?"

Harry scratches his head with his glasses.

"Without running the all the numbers, I don't know exactly, but I'd ballpark at least $100,000. You've got to lease a space which is going to take money, you're going to have to stock inventory and I'm assuming you're going to need staff even if it's a couple part-time employee. And, I haven't even begun to touch your marketing costs and the fact that you need to be able to pay yourself. Are you sure this is what you want to do? It's probably not too late to go back to the agency if you want. At least that's stable."

I am so sick of people doubting me. Why does everyone think this is so crazy?

"No, Harry, she's doing this," Allison defends. "Tal has waited a long time for this and she has already given up so much for this dream. It's time."

That's why I love Allison. It is so great to have an ally when I felt like the world is up against me. I mouth a big "thank you" to her as Harry just sits there shaking his head. I can't fault him . He is a practical guy like Tony so financially, this doesn't make sense to him. He can only see what is in black and white, but I have a big vision for my future.

"Okay, do you have something to put toward this? Any savings? Collateral?"

"Well, yea, I do have a few thousand in the bank, in my savings but it is not going to scratch the surface of what I need."

"How much?"

"About $20,000."

"But Tal, you're also out of work right now. You don't want to exhaust all of your savings when you are not bringing in an active income," Allison says.

I think of Zack's offer to help, but there's still a large chasm to reach my goal

"You're going to have to get a loan," Harry says.

"Okay," I say, ready to move forward and do whatever I need to do, "what is the first step? The only loan I have experience in is my mortgage."

"Well, for one, you've got to write that business plan."

"Okay," I say.

I don't have the first clue how to write a business plan.

Harry puts his glasses back on and studies me.

"Have you ever written a business plan before?"

"No," I say, shaking my head.

"Okay," he says, "I think I have a book that I can loan you. There are people that we could hire to do this for you, but I honestly think this would be a good exercise for you to flesh out your business in more detail. Quite frankly, you can't hire someone to write your business plan if you don't have full clarity on what you want to do first and there are still some things you need to learn yourself. Plus, I think you are competent enough to write your own plan. You're a smart girl which is why I'm surprised that you want to take on such a risk at this point in your career. Allison told me that you turned down a partnership with the agency to do this." He raises an inquisitive eyebrow.

"Yes, I did. Harry, I'm doing this" I say, not flinching.

"You're not worried that this won't work out, about the possibility of failing? Have you looked up the failure rate of startup businesses? Most of them don't make it. And, don't you have a young daughter?"

"Harry!" Allison yells, "Enough!"

"It's okay, Allison," I say, "Harry's scare tactics don't work on me. I know what I'm doing. I understand that everyone is not going to understand why I'm doing this and won't hop on the bandwagon.

Trust me, I get that. But this is something I need to do. I understand that failure is a possibility but I'd rather risk failure than live the rest of my life in regret."

Harry concedes, especially since Allison is now flashing him dirty looks.

"Okay," he says, throwing his hands up as he gets up from the table and grabs his briefcase, "I never said I wasn't going to support you. I'd like you to succeed because I can tell you are passionate about this, but I want you to know that it's a big undertaking. Be prepared for all outcomes."

"Thank you. I appreciate that, but I'm okay. Really."

"Alright. Well, I'll get that book to you by tomorrow, so you can start working on your business plan. My advice to you is to take your time with this and do it right. It's your gateway to funding so it has to show the bank that your idea is profitable. You're going to need to do some research on things like the designers and manufacturers that you want to work with, and the cost associated with that. You will also need to include the cost to lease space. Utilize the Small Business Administration. There are a lot of resources there about building your business plan as well. Call me if you have any questions. I will help any way I can. I mean that."

Harry hands me his card, leans in and kisses Allison's cheek, and leaves the café.

After he's walked out the door, Allison clutches my hand.

"I'm so sorry," she says. "He can be such a jerk sometimes."

I shrug it off.

"It's OK. He didn't say anything that wasn't true."

"Regardless, he shouldn't have been so negative."

"Allison, he's right. I am going against the grain doing this. I'm scared as hell. The last time I remember being this scared, I was becoming a mother for the first time."

"That didn't turn out too bad now, did it?" she smiles.

I reflect on my precious girl and what she means to me. She has changed me for the better. I love being her mom.

"Are you thinking of backing out?"

"It's funny. The logical side of me is saying, 'Tal, what are you doing? This is crazy.' Nothing about this decision makes sense. But, my heart is saying something totally different. When I think about this, I feel so exhilarated. Allison, I've never wanted something so bad before."

"Then, let's do it."

୫

I go home and help Jasmine with her homework, cook dinner and put her to bed. I have some homework of my own to get started on. If I want to see this happen, I need capital and that means I am going to have to make friends with the bank. I must show them that this venture is worthwhile and that it is going to make some money.

I go into my office downstairs and start to do some research. I know Harry is going to get that book to me tomorrow, but I do not want to delay. I am anxious to get this process started.

I sit in front of my computer and pull up the Small Business Administration website. I am amazed at the wealth of information. I don't know why I hadn't t checked this out earlier. I also see that there are loans available here too. I click on the tab, Business Plans.

I learn that there are many components to a business plan. It is a lot more than just stating what your business is. I am going to have to do a market analysis and prove that my business model will be soluble. I am going to have to research the competition and determine that there is a need for the products I'll be providing.

I need a deadline to complete this. I give myself two months to complete my business plan before meeting with a banker. I am excited and anxious at the same time.

TURN TO PAGE 129 TO CONTINUE TALIA'S JOURNEY TO START HER BOUTIQUE.

After popping a few Benadryl, I am finally able to doze off. The revolting sound of my alarm hurts my ears. 6:30 AM.

I groan and roll out of bed. Today, I will be telling Tim my decision. Taking this job makes sense. After much deliberation, I realize that the best decision for me is to take this position to give me the leverage and the tools I need to open my boutique. Starting my boutique is still my goal and focus and I promise myself to never let go of that. After all, it is the only reason why I am considering this partnership. I think Tim's will introduce me to some key connections that will make my dream real in the biggest way possible. My shoulders are much lighter this morning. I've removed the huge boulder that has been weighing me down and I have a different air of confidence about me. I am about to become partner of the agency. This is huge! For the first time in a long time, excitement washes over me. Now, I have a plan. This is good.

❧

I walk into the office, a smile on my face, confident about the future that lies ahead. No more walking in with my head down, ignoring my staff. I am about to gain ownership in this company, and it is time I start acting like it.

"Good morning," I beam to my team as I walk toward my office.

I'm greeted with some smiles from my team and trepidation from others. Allison follows me into my office.

"You've got a pep in your step this morning," she closes the door behind her.

Sitting my laptop bag in my chair behind my desk, I face my friend squarely.

"I made a decision."

Allison's eyes brighten.

"Great! When do you give notice?"

I sit down next to my friend in front of my desk.

"I'm not exactly giving notice."

Allison is taken aback.

"I'm going to take Tim's offer."

Allison is disappointed, I can tell.

"Please, don't look at me like that. I've agonized over this for so long. I really feel this is the best decision for me right now. That does not mean that I do not want to open my boutique. That is still within my plans. Please, Allison, don't for a second think I've given up on my dreams. They are, in fact, very vivid. That's the reason I chose to accept this position. I concluded that no matter what decisions you make in your life, there's always a price to pay. My price for my dream of owning my boutique is taking the job, because it will afford me resources and will open doors that I don't already have access to. This is a good thing," I explain.

Allison grabs my hand, encouragingly.

"Sweetie, I will support you no matter what you choose to do. I just want to make sure you're happy, and one thing that has been evident for a long time, to me at least, is that you've not been happy here. You're longing for something more, and I thought this boutique was it for you."

"It is, Allison. That is clear. I'm just willing to make this sacrifice to get what I want."

Allison shakes her head.

"That's just it, Talia. How many people get a big promotion offer like this and view it as a sacrifice? Did you ever think that the simple fact that you view it this way is a sign that you might be ready to go your own way?"

"I want to, Allison. I really do. I'm just not ready. This is the best path for me now. Yes…yes." I am convincing myself now, "It's what I need to do. As a matter of fact, I'm going to tell Tim right now."

I walk around the desk and pick up the envelope that has haunted me for the last couple of weeks. The ink of my signature is still wet from this morning. I know Allison does not necessarily agree with my reasoning for doing this, but she will understand in time.

"You have been the most supportive friend that I could ever ask for, Allison. I will continue to need your support as I move forward with this decision. Understand that this has not been easy for me."

I hug her, open the door to my office, and turn back before going down the hall.

"Don't let me forget what's important," I say.

Staying back in my office, Allison seems frozen in place.

"I fear you already have."

⁂

"Tim."

I knock lightly on his office door.

"Come in," he bellows.

Tim is sitting at his desk typing away on his laptop. Looking up at me, he smiles.

"Hi Talia. See what you get to look forward to as partner? It seems your work never ends."

He gestures to the mountain of paperwork that sits on his desk next to his computer.

Walking further into Tim's office, I'm ready to give him what he's been waiting over two weeks for, my decision.

"That's what I came here to discuss with you, Tim. I made my decision." With that I lay the manila envelope on his desk and sit down in the one of the chairs in front of his desk to gauge his response.

Tim sits quietly, studying me. You can cut the tension in the room with a knife. Finally, he picks up the envelope and pulls out my signed agreement.

A sardonic smile glides across his face as he realizes he's won.

The wider his smile gets, the wider I feel the crevice grow from me and my dream.

"Talia, you've made the right decision," he says. "You're going to make a fine addition to my executive team. I'm looking forward to showing you the ropes and preparing you to take this whole operation over yourself one day."

Pasting on a reciprocal smile, "Thank you for the opportunity, Mr. Stevens."

Standing up and walking around his desk, Tim responds, "We're partners now, Talia. Enough with the formalities. Please, call me Tim."

"Oh, right...Tim," I respond uncomfortably. I extend my hand to seal our deal.

Instead of taking my hand, Tim shocks me with an awkward hug.

"I'd like you to start in your new role right away. There's a lot to do. Bradley moved out of his office a few weeks ago, so that big office next door is yours. We'll be working closely together so the proximity is convenient and it's also an upgrade from your existing office."

This is moving faster than I thought. I expected more time ease into this role.

"Sir, what about my current position? We're currently in the middle of a campaign. I don't want to just abandon my team."

"Of course, of course," Tim waves his hand flippantly, "we'll slowly work to phase you out of your creative director role while we work on finding a suitable replacement for you. In the meantime, I still want you to move offices and maintain both roles for a little while. You will be working some heavy hours for a while, but welcome to the life of being a partner. I promise, you'll be well compensated for the time spent."

"Thank you, Mr. Stevens – I mean Tim. I won't let you down."

"I know you won't," his eyes are down, and he's already resumed his work as I walk out of his office.

What have I gotten myself into?

&.

When I get home this evening, I feel a little less confident and sure of myself than I did when I'd left in the morning. I made my decision, but I am afraid that I just pushed my dream further out of reach. Jasmine is upstairs in her room doing her homework and I head into the kitchen to work on dinner. My phone vibrates on the counter, startling me.

I pick it up.

"Hi sweetheart," a familiar voice chimes, a voice I really need to hear right now.

"Hey Tony."

"What are you doing right now?"

Looking at the frozen chicken breast in my freezer, I realize I'm not about to cook dinner.

"Well," I say, "I was about to cook dinner, but it looks like pizza might be on the menu tonight."

"Would you like some company? I'll get the pizza. I've some exciting news to share with you and I'd rather share with you in person rather than over the phone. As a matter of fact, I'll do better than pizza. I'll pick up some dinner from that Thai place you and Jazz like so much. Is it a date?"

Glad to have some extra company tonight, I agree.

"It's a date."

Tony arrives in a festive mood. Jasmine, of course, is happy to see him because she loves spending time with him. We have a great dinner together, some good laughs and end the night with Jasmine falling asleep to the tunes of *Frozen* on our Blu-ray player. After I tuck her into bed, I come back downstairs, exhausted, more mentally than physically. The task of making the decision about this partnership has literally wiped me out. Tony can sense my exhaustion and meets me in my living room with a glass of wine. Bless this man!

"You look like you've had a long day," he walks behind the couch and begins to knead my shoulders.

I sit in silence for a moment, relishing in the pampering. It feels so good.

Finally feeling relaxed, I speak.

"It has been a long few weeks for me, but you were excited about something when we spoke on the phone, so what is it? Go ahead. Spill the beans."

Tony walks around the couch to join me, eyes dancing. He's adorable when he's excited.

"My firm just asked me to be partner."

I jump up and throw my arms around him. Partnership has been part of Tony's career plan, but not this soon.

"That's great news, Tony. Were you expecting it?"

"That's the thing. Not really. I mean – of course it is something I aspire towards, but I did not see anything like this happening for a few years at least. I've been very happy at this firm, but they have a very strong leadership team, so I did not even know if partner would be an option here."

"How did it all happen? Tell me."

"The partners called me into their office this afternoon before lunch. I'll admit, at first, I was a little nervous. I know that I do an excellent job but anytime all the partners summon you, you just tend think the worst. Anyway, they called me in and went on and on about my performance over the last few years. They told me that I was the future of this firm and that they'd like to work together to groom me to run the firm with them. So, they offered me a junior partner position that comes with a raise and several other perks, including stock and a percentage ownership in the firm."

"Wow, that sounds like a pretty sweet deal, Tony. How long did they give you to make the decision?"

Tony shakes his head.

"I didn't need any time. I accepted and signed on the dotted line today and then all of the partners took me out to a big, fancy lunch to celebrate."

I sit quietly for a moment. To Tony it must feel like a lifetime.

"Is everything okay? Did you not want me to take this position?"

"No-no, it's great, Tony. I'm so happy for you. It's just that, making this decision just came so easily to you. But, for me, I've been agonizing over my decision for so long. It has literally tormented me."

Tony takes my hand in his.

"We talked about this. You know my take on it and the game plan I think you should follow."

I squeeze his hand.

"I know, and I understand. So, I signed the papers and accepted the partnership with Tim today."

Tony grabs me and twirls me around in the air.

"This is fantastic," he says, setting me back on the ground. "The timing couldn't be any better. You and I are in the best places of our careers, which is why now is the perfect time."

"Perfect time? Perfect for what?"

Tony drops to one knee and I'm ready to hyperventilate.

"Talia, I know this is not the perfect atmosphere with candles and a big dinner like we both dreamed, but the time just seems right. I've been planning to do this for weeks now, but you've been so tense and stressed. I wanted you to come to a happy resolution so that we can start the process of building our life together. I love you so much, and I want nothing more than to spend the rest of my life with you. Will you please do me the honor of becoming my wife?"

The tears are streaming down my face. He caught me completely off guard and I don't realized the time that has passed by.

"Talia?" Tony asks looking concerned as he presents me with a beautiful 2.5 carat princess cut diamond. It is beautiful. Flawless. I struggled with my last big decision, but this one comes easily.

"Yes."

※

One year later….

Tony and I have been married for three months now. We planned our wedding quickly in anticipation of the harsh demands of our new positions. Everything is still a blur. So much has happened in the last year. Tony and I got married. I sold the townhouse and Tony and I bought our first home together. The picture-perfect dream. A beautiful brick, transitional on a corner lot with a picket fence. What more could a girl want, right? Except that I spend less time in my new home and more at my new job. My new role as partner at the agency turned out to be more taxing that I ever expected. Tim is pulling me in all directions and his big ambitions to grow our agency presence has resulted in me traveling extensively over the past six months. I think I remember being home maybe three nights in the past two weeks. Things haven't been much different for Tony. Taking on the role of junior partner for him not only meant more responsibility but he also took on a lot of the tasks that the senior partners did not want to do since he was in training. He isn't traveling as much as I am, thank God! But, it isn't uncommon for him to be working on his laptop until nearly two in the morning on projects he's been assigned. We are newlyweds, but we've barely spent any time together in the last year. I miss my daughter. With all the working, neither of us has much time to spend with her so she spends a lot of time with the sitter. Realizing the demands of work, Zack has been a God-send, coming in town more frequently than usual to give our daughter some quality time with one of her parents.

As I am burning the midnight oil, once again in the office, Tim stops in to check on me.

"Talia," he says, interrupting my mode as I am working through a multitude of projects.

Glancing up barely from my laptop, I say, "Tim, hi," as I keep on typing.

Walking into the office and closing the door, Tim sits across from me at my desk.

"Talia," he says, concerned, "I think you need to slow down."

The typing stops, and I look up at him. I am tired, but there is just so much to do.

"Tim, I need to finish this report by 8 am." Picking up another pile from my desk, "And this presentation is due to Caruthers by next Wednesday. I was going to book my flight to deliver it before I left here tonight."

Tim glances at his watch.

"Talia, darling, it's 9:30. Go home."

"Tim, I can't go home until I…" Tim interrupts me before I can finish my plea.

"Talia, seriously, go home. As a matter of fact, I want you to take a few days off."

"Tim, are you firing me?" I say, feeling worried.

"Of course not, Talia. Quite the contrary, you are my most valued asset at this firm, my partner. You're burning the candle at both ends. You've been going full force since you accepted this partnership, and it's not that I don't appreciate it, I can clearly see signs of burn out. I need to protect my interests. You need a break."

Though I don't really want to admit it, Tim is right. I am exhausted and even as I was getting ready this morning, I could see the dark circles setting in under my eyes from fatigue.

"When is the last time you had a nice dinner with your new husband or a play date with your daughter?" Tim asks.

I can't even remember the last time we've spent any quality time together since the wedding. We took an abbreviated honeymoon because we both needed to get back to work for our new positions.

I'm at a loss for words.

"I asked you to be my partner because you're the best and the brightest, but if you work yourself into a stupor, you're of no use to me. I need you to take some time to recharge."

I know Tim is right. I do need a break, but I don't see how that is going to happen.

"Tim, I do appreciate what you're saying, and I do think you're right. But, how do I do that when there is just so much to do? How can you expect me to take time off when I need to fly to L.A. next week for a presentation? We can't afford for me to leave."

Tim waves his hand in the air.

"We'll figure it out. If I can't go, we have capable people on our team that you can delegate to. But right now I'm ordering you to take a few mental health days. This is not a negotiation. Now go."

I feel a rush of relief and calm come over me. Tim is right. I need this. It feels good to be able to hand some responsibility back over to him even for just a few days.

I start to shut down my laptop and gather my things.

"Ok, Ok, I get the hint. I'm going."

Tim gets up and walks to my door.

"Plus, I have a global deal I'm working on ,so we may have to travel to Prague next month. I need you fresh."

I run my hands through my hair in exasperation. This job is running me ragged.

৯

After just two days from the office, I feel refreshed and wide-eyed. Tony has not received the gift of a few days off, so he works his usual long hours. We are scheduled to go out to dinner as a family tonight, so in the meantime, I enjoy some quality time with Jazz. When I ask her what she wants to do, she immediately tells me that she wants to go out for ice cream. After hanging out at the mall and the park most of the day, we decide that the perfect prequel to our dinner with Tony is an ice cream cone.

After grabbing our ice cream, Jasmine and I take a stroll past some of the downtown shops, soaking in the sunshine of the day.

As we pass the different shops, each one trendier than the next, Jasmine stops at one of them excitedly.

"Mommy, when are you going to get me all of those free clothes from your shop that you promised?"

My shop? Oh yeah! Now, I remember, I did want to open a shop of my own. I investigate the shop in front of us, suddenly feeling an ache in my heart, but realizing that I may have reached a point of no return.

I've buried my dream once again.

"Someday sweetheart. Someday."

A DREAM DEFERRED. THE END.

A couple of weeks later, Zack comes down to see Jasmine like we'd discussed. I started working part-time at a local boutique to get some hands-on experience while earning some extra money. Although I am living off savings and Zack is helping me out, I do not want to exhaust it completely. The money I make working at the shop is nothing to write home about, but it helps cover some home expenses and gives me some experience working in a real shop.

It's Saturday and Zack has taken Jasmine out for the day. I'm working, but told them that I'll be able to meet them for dinner when I get off.

I enjoy working for the boutique. I am learning a lot about things I want to do and things I don't, and it is a lot less stressful than working at the agency. I am finishing up with a customer around 6:30, just a few minutes before I am due to clock out and catch up with Zack and Jasmine for dinner, when I see a familiar face walk past the shop.

He notices me too because he doubles back and walks in the store. It is Tony. Time stands still for a moment. God, I forgot how handsome he is.

"Talia, aren't you going to greet our customer?" my manager smiles at Tony.

I walk over to him. Still no words come out of my mouth. It has been a few weeks since our breakup. He calls numerous times, but I don't answer. I need a clean break. It's better this way. As I stand in front of him gazing at his handsome face, all my feelings rush back. I'm still in love with this man.

"Hey stranger," he says.

"Hi," my voice is barely a whisper.

"You haven't returned any of my calls," he stands in a tailored suit, hands in his pockets.

"I thought it was easier for us both that way."

He takes a step closer.

"I've been sick without you."

"Tony," I hold up my hand and take another step back, trying to keep my distance, "I'm working."

He takes another step closer and reaches for my hand.

"Can we talk?"

I look back toward my manager who is watching our every move.

'Go ahead,' she mouths, grin on her face.

I walk outside, reluctantly.

A light brown tendril of my hair falls to my face. He smooths it back behind my ear, his hand lingering on my cheek. I don't brush his hand away. His familiar touch feels good.

"I've missed you," he says, "why haven't you been returning my calls?"

"Tony, you know why."

He backs away, exasperated.

"You just decide it's over and that's it? After all we've been through together?"

"Tony, I'm going down a path you don't want to follow. How can we build a future on opposite sides?" I plead.

"Tal, I still love you," he says.

"I love you too, Tony," I say, "but I've come to the realization that love by itself is just not enough. I need your support. I need you to believe in me, and even as I look in your eyes, I can tell that has not changed."

"Then help me to understand," he says, grabbing my hand, "don't throw away what we have. It means too much to both of us."

My heart is breaking all over again. My feelings are still too fresh.

"Tony, I can't do this."

"Because you still love me," he says, "why do we need to be miserable? Let's fix this right now."

He reaches in his pocket and pulls out the beautiful diamond ring that I'd given back to him.

He gets down on one knee.

"Talia, be my wife."

Why is he doing this? Everyone in the store stops what they are doing to peer outside at us. Passersby stop in their tracks to observe Tony's romantic gesture. And I am uncomfortable.

"Tony, get up."

"Not until you give me an answer."

"You're not going to like my answer because it has not changed. You can't come to my job and pull this and think you can manipulate me into saying yes."

"Manipulate you?" Tony says, getting up, "you just told me that you loved me."

"I also told you that love by itself is not enough."

"What's your plan then, Talia? What are you going to do? You're working in a retail store for God's sake. You used to be a creative director, remember that?"

"Yes, Tony, I remember. And, if you remember, it was not what I wanted. You never supported that."

"Talia, I can't support what I don't understand."

Damn, here come the waterworks.

"I don't know how to make you understand," I tell him.

"Everything okay here?"

The familiar voice suspends our conversation. Zack and Jasmine are standing behind me. Talking to Tony, I've lost track of time. We are supposed to meet for dinner.

"Tony!" Jasmine yells as she jumps into his arms.

Still concerned about me, Zack gently grabs my elbow.

"Are you okay?" he whispers.

"I will be," I say. "Tony was just leaving."

But Jasmine detains him.

"Where have you been?" she demands.

"Uh," Tony says, struggling to find the words, rubbing the back of his neck.

I rescue him.

"He's been busy with work, sweetheart," I say. "Now let's go or we're going to be later for dinner."

Tony still isn't ready to let us go. Zack has his attention now.

"I don't believe we've formally met, I'm Tony," he says, extending his hand.

"Zack," he says, shaking Tony's hand.

"This is my daddy," Jasmine says, proudly clinging to his leg.

Why do I feel like I'm in a love triangle? Tony standing there in his tailored suit, and my country boy, Zack in well-worn jeans and a t-shirt. He's really wearing those jeans.

"We really have to get going," I say, "we have dinner reservations."

I turn around and start walking before Tony even had a chance to respond.

Zack, Jasmine and I have a great dinner as a family. Jasmine is on cloud nine because her parents are together. I try to stay focused. Seeing Tony this evening rocked me, but I'm trying to keep my composure. Zack keeps flashing me concerned looks during dinner. He's worried about me, I know. He's such a sweet guy, and I forgot how damn cute he was. He's letting his beard grow in again. I used to tell him back in high school that I loved him clean shaven, but as I glance across the table at him, I'm finding the gruff look very sexy.

Zack shoots me a quizzical smile. Dammit, I'm staring.

I shake it off and just smile back, averting my eyes from Zack immediately after.

After dinner, we return to the townhouse and Jasmine begs Zack to tuck her in before he heads back to his hotel for the evening.

I am glad to have a few minutes to myself while he is upstairs with her. I am on an emotional roller coaster. I want to get back with Tony so badly but not at the expense of my dream. Why can't he just support me? I'm not asking that much, am I? And, then I realize these feelings creeping in about Zack. What's that about? I stared at his ass when he was walking away after the Tony incident. He does have a nice ass, but why was I even looking? What's going on with me?

Zack disturbs my thoughts when he comes down the stairs and pulls up a chair.

"Ready to talk?"

I smile tentatively.

"I wear my emotions on my sleeve, don't I?"

"Maybe not to everyone else, but to me, yes," he says, "I take it the conversation with the boyfriend didn't go too well."

"He's not my boyfriend anymore."

"Okay. He doesn't seem to believe that," Zack says slowly. "I think he might have even been jealous of me."

"That's ridiculous," I say, laughing.

"Is it really?" Zack asks. "We do have a child together."

"Yes, do we do, but I don't know if he was jealous. He just wants things to be like they were. And, Zack, I do too. More than anything. We kind of just reached the point of no return in our relationship. How can I marry someone who doesn't believe in my dreams?"

Zack places a compassionate hand over mine. Goosebumps run up my arm. That's new.

"Tal, I get it."

"I still love him," I say, as tears well up in my eyes and I pull my hand way to wipe my tears, "how can I move on when he keeps showing up like this?"

"He clearly still loves you, too."

"I told him that love isn't enough."

"Ouch," Zack says.

"What?"

"It's just a painful reminder of how we parted ways. I've always loved you, Tal, you know that. I could never fault you for wanting a better life for you and our daughter. One thing I know about you is that when you want something you go after it with all you have, and you get it."

Suddenly, I feel the sting of our past. Zack has always been a great guy, but he is a small-town guy. He wasn't comfortable venturing into the big city but always supported me in my endeavors, even though it meant the end of our relationship. At first, I think maybe he is taking Tony's side, but now I realize that he empathizes with him. Did he say he still loves me?

"Am I a bad person? Zack, is love enough?" I question.

Zack ponders my question for a while.

"I don't know, Tal. I guess for some, it might be. Relationships are hard. They require compromise and working together, and I guess at some point, you must give up part of yourself. That's part of the vulnerability of being in love."

"You think I should give up my dream for the sake of me and Tony's relationship?" I ask.

"No, I didn't say that."

"Then what are you saying because I am confused?"

Zack rubs his forehead.

"I don't know, Tal. I can tell you love this guy and you're hurting, but honestly, you should never be forced to choose between the man you love and your dream. There are consequences on either side."

"Like me resenting him if I choose him over my dream?"

Zack nods.

"Or suffer the broken heart of letting him go?"

Zack walks over and pulls me in for a much-needed hug. All of a sudden, it feels awkward. I'm feeling something I thought died a long time ago. I ignore my conscience and enjoy the warmth of his touch.

"It won't always hurt this bad," he says.

I pull back a little bit from his embrace.

"Are you speaking from experience?"

Zack walks away from me and grabs a stool in the kitchen.

"Tonight is not about me; it's about you," he says, "what do you feel in your heart, Tal?"

"My heart says it's over."

It hurts so much to say it out loud.

"Are you sure? You seem to be holding on pretty tight."

"That's because I just saw him for the first time in a couple of weeks. Not seeing him somehow helped me cope. Seeing him today, I just wanted to run into his arms and for things be like they used to be. But they can't."

"Do you think he could ever support you?"

"That's just it, Zack," I say, "if he even showed an inkling of support, we'd still be together. He keeps telling me that he doesn't understand. And, I don't know how to make him understand. He doesn't want this for me and I don't think he believes I can do this. That's what hurts most of all. I'm not even 100% sure I can do this, but I've got to try. I don't want to live the rest of my life in regret."

"It sounds to me like Tony likes to play things safe," Zack says.

"Very."

"So, it's over?"

"Yes."

"What's next?"

"I've got to figure out how to make this happen. I need to prove to him and myself that I can do this. I met with a finance guy recently and he told me that I need to put together a business plan so that I can get funding. I don't have enough in savings to just start a shop so that's where I am. I've started working on my plan, but it requires a lot of research. I hope to be done in another couple of weeks. Then, I'm going to meet with my money guy again before approaching the bank."

Zack leans back looking impressed.

"I can tell by the look on your face that you're impressed," I say. "Zack, I've got to make this work. I gave up a really great opportunity to do this. Yes, I know on the outside, it doesn't seem to make a lot of sense, but to me, it's all I've ever really dreamed of. There's a lot riding on this. I've got a child to think of now. It's not just me."

"We've got a child," Zack corrects me, "and you have my full support. My offer to help you still stands. I believe in you, Tal. Like I said, when you set your mind to something, it's already done. And, this, well this just makes sense for you. Remember, I've known you since we were kids, so I understand why you want to do this."

I run over to Zack and give him another a big hug. Damn whatever unresolved feelings that are lingering. I need him right now.

"I can't begin to tell you how much your support means to me. You and Allison have been God-sends. When you decide to leave your job after being offered a lucrative partnership to pursue opening a clothing boutique, friends and family are not lining up to support you. My parents think I'm crazy and well, you know Tony's point of view. My list of cheerleaders is very short."

"The girl I remember from high school never cared about what others thought," Zack reminds me.

"I don't," I say, pacing the floor, "but it sure does wear on a girl's self-image after a while."

"Tal, you are capable. Just know that."

He looks down at his watch.

"It's getting late. I should head back to the hotel," Zack heads toward the door.

"Okay."

"You feel a little better now?"

I smile.

"I always feel better after talking to you."

"Good," he says, "I'm in town a couple more days, so I can arrange to pick Jazz up from school tomorrow if you like."

"Okay," I say, "I'll let the school know."

Zack gets ready to leave.

"Zack, did it hurt?" I ask.

"Did what hurt?"

"Letting me go?"

He lowers his head for a moment and then gazes into my eyes.

"Like hell, Tal."

My cheeks flush. If I were reading anything into the moment, I'd say he still loves me, and I…

"Good night, Tal."

"Good night, Zack."

I close the door and walk back into the kitchen. I reminisce back to the old days when Zack and I were a couple. We were good together. We just went on separate paths in our lives, I guess, much like Tony. Except Zack has always been supportive of whatever I want to do even if it doesn't fit within his own plan. Tony, on the other hand, just can't see or try to understand why I am choosing to go down this path. What hurts the most is he isn't willing to face the challenges with me. Why does he always have to play things so safe? Despite my run in with Tony, I feel so much better after spending some time with Zack. We're more in sync now than we've ever been. There's a saying, when one door closes, another opens. Is Zack my open door?

Time to get some sleep. I have a lot of work ahead of me on this business plan and I want to make sure that I have this thing wrapped up by my deadline so I can start building my dream.

*

3 weeks later

I sit in the cold lobby of the bank waiting for the banker to see me. The last few weeks have been a whirlwind with all the remaining research I needed to do to complete my business plan. This is my dream, my livelihood. I want to make sure that I do this right. Every night for the last couple of weeks, I found myself up until midnight or later working on my business plan. I followed the format in the book Harry gave me as a template. Once I got the go ahead from Harry that everything looked good, I went to a local print shop and had it bound and copied to present to the banker. The banker that Harry suggested has done a lot of business with startups, so I am hoping to be their next investment. Harry has been gracious enough to come to my appointment with me.

"Nervous?" he asks, as I sit in the lobby chair tapping my leg.

"Yes," I reply, my voice a little shaky. "I just have so much riding on this, Harry. If this doesn't work for me, I don't know what I'm going to do."

"Talia Cooper."

Game on.

Harry lays a comforting hand on my shoulder.

"Calm down," he says, "just present the information you've prepared. This is the first step in a long process."

I nod, get up and walk in the office. Harry follows.

"Good morning Ms. Cooper. I'm Janet Lawson. I'll be meeting with you today."

I lean across the table and shake her hand.

"Nice to meet you, Ms. Lawson."

She shoots a curt nod to Harry.

"Harry."

"Janet, good to see you. I'm advising Ms. Cooper on this venture."

I'm hoping their familiarity will work in my favor. This woman looks tough as nails.

She smiles, slightly.

"Great, I'm looking forward to seeing what you two cooked up. Shall we get started? Do you have a business plan for me?"

"Yes, I do," I say, reaching into my briefcase retrieving my perfectly bound copy and handing it to her.

There is silence as she begins to read through the business plan. I sit there nervously for what feels like an eternity.

Janet finally breaks the silence.

"Ms. Cooper, do you have any collateral for this loan?"

I had not considered any collateral when I walked in. Harry and I have not discussed that. I am asking for $250,000. Harry says that is the baseline figure of what I will need to cover all the expenses of the shop, including rent, staff and merchandise until I start to turn a profit.

"Uh, no Ms. Lawson. I had not really considered that. Is it necessary to secure this loan?"

She continues to flip through the pages of my business plan before answering me.

"Most likely," she says. "Offering collateral helps minimize our risk here at the bank. Do you own any assets?"

"I own a townhome and my car," I say, perking up a bit.

She continues to look through the business plan.

"Do you have any information on those assets in here?" she asks.

"No, but I'd be happy to put that together for you."

Janet closes the pages of the business plan and looks at me sternly.

"Ms. Cooper, why do you want to open a clothing boutique? You have a very impressive résumé and background that would lend itself to something in the creative world like an advertising or graphic design."

I chuckle.

"Did I say something funny, Ms. Cooper?" she asks, lowering her glasses.

This woman is everything that would intimidate you about meeting with a bank lender. Uptight, shrewd and did I saw uptight?

"Well, kind of," I say, looking her in the eyes, "you see that's why I'm here. I've been in the creative, graphic design business for quite some time. And, yes, you're correct, I have the experience there and I'm very good at it, but I've lost my passion for it. That's what's led me to this point, sitting in front of you here today. This boutique has been a dream inside of me since I was a little kid. It's hard to put it into exact words, but it's what I was born to do."

Now it is Ms. Lawson's turn to chuckle under her breath.

She takes her glasses all the way off this time.

"I admire your ambition, Ms. Cooper. Unfortunately, that alone doesn't finance or secure the success of your business. I can't extend a loan to you based on what you feel you were born to do. You have to understand that."

Slowly I feel my dream slipping away.

"What about my business plan? Doesn't that count for anything?" I ask desperately.

Ms. Lawson starts to thumb through my business plan once again.

"Your business plan is a vital component in our decision, yes, but at first glance, this document is very shallow and does not provide me with the level of detail I need. There are no solid numbers or vision for where this business is going. You just haven't given me enough. While you may be able to use your home as some form of collateral, your business experience is not extensive enough to show that you can effectively run this type of business and make it profitable."

"You just told me that I had an impressive background," I plead.

"Yes, in graphic design," Ms. Lawson clarifies. "If you were here to tell me you wanted to open your own graphic design firm or advertising agency, that would be much more plausible given your level of experience. But you're telling me you want to open a clothing boutique with no credibility in this field. This is a totally different business model that your experience doesn't lend itself to."

"I recently started working at a clothing boutique," I defend myself. "Does that count for anything?"

Ms. Lawson admires my ambition.

"No, honey," she says, placing a comforting hand on my arm, "not enough to get you a $250,000 loan."

I don't feel comforted. I feel robbed. How can I have come this far, making the sacrifices I've made, only to be denied before I even get started?

I just realize Harry has been here the entire time, but he's remained silent. Everything is on the line. I need him to say something.

I flash him a looking, pleading, "help me."

Harry leans forward in his chair.

"Janet, this is something Talia is extremely passionate about. She's given up a lot to pursue this dream. If you cannot give her a loan today, can you at least make some suggestions of what she needs to do to move forward. She just needs some guidance."

I mouth a thank you to Harry.

Ms. Lawson leans back in her chair to think about my next steps. Then, she leans forward and looks at me.

"I know you're excited about pursuing your dream, and I don't want to discourage you from doing it," Ms. Lawson advises, "but you are going to have to be more patient. Businesses are not built overnight Ms. Cooper. I'd advise that you build up your résumé in the retail area so that you can bring some expertise to the table. That will help your cause. I'd also suggest that you spend more time developing your business plan, more clearly outlining how you see this business succeeding."

"How long do you think all of this will take, Ms. Lawson?" My tone is impatient. "I don't have the luxury of building another career just so that I can start my own business in this industry."

Ms. Lawson shrugs her shoulders.

"I don't know, maybe a year. What you need to do is prove to the bank that you're not only passionate about your new venture but that you're knowledgeable about it as well. If you don't have the knowledge yet, then you need to at least have someone on your board that can advise you toward your success. Does that make sense?"

"Yes, it does."

"I'm sorry that I cannot help you today, Ms. Cooper. You have a lot of passion and fire in your eyes. You must realize that I sit across from many aspiring business owners with passion and fire every day. Those that I took a chance on but did not have a clear vision about what they were doing and what they truly wanted to accomplish didn't last. Passion is great and needed when starting a business, but it alone cannot get you from point A to point B. You've got to have a vision and you need to organize that vision into a plan to achieve your goals. That's what you need to work on, and when you've done that, Talia, your possibilities will be endless."

Harry stands and extends his hand to Ms. Lawson.

"Thank you for your time, Janet. We'll work on these areas and will definitely be back when we are ready."

I stand and shake her hand as well, and we exit the bank.

"That couldn't have gone any worse," I say, defeated.

"I disagree," Harry says, sounding encouraged, "at least she told you what you need to work on, and you can follow her advice and come back later. You have to admit, we did throw that business plan together and while I did the best I could with it, we needed more time to develop your full vision and plan like she said."

"Yea, but Harry, a year? Do I have that kind of time? I just quit my job and gave up a partnership offer in my firm for this. Jasmine and I are still living off my savings and I don't know if it can carry us that much longer. We need to get this thing started now."

Harry stops to face me.

"You've taken great risks to go after something you believe in, something you believe is your true dream. I admire that. Not too many people have the courage to do what you've done. But, to think that this journey will be quick and easy is a foolish assumption. Haven't you ever heard that the road to success is an uphill battle all the way? You should know this more than most people, coming to Atlanta to make a better life for you and Jasmine, you didn't start out with the creative director job at the agency, right?"

I shake my head.

"Right, you had to fight the whole way, and I'm sure you ran into some bumps along the way. This is no different. Patience is a virtue. Take what Janet told you to heart and press forward. Don't hang your head in defeat."

"You're right, Harry."

"I know," he says, "now let's go catch up with Allison and Jasmine."

We hop in Harry's car and head to my house where Allison and Jasmine are waiting for us.

As I walk in the door, I breathe a sigh of relief. The familiar surroundings of home are comforting.

I walk into the living room with Harry to find Jasmine and Allison lounging on the couch watching TV.

Jasmine lights up when she sees me.

"Mommy," she screams, running over to me.

I wrap my arms around her. God, I love this kid. I hope I haven't ruined things for her by quitting my job.

"How'd it go?" she asks, big brown eyes gleaming.

"It went okay," I fake. "Why don't you go back in the room and watch TV? Mommy needs to talk to Auntie Allison for a bit okay?"

"Okay," she says, kissing me on the cheek and running back to the couch.

Allison reads my body language.

"That bad huh?" she says as she walks into the kitchen to join me and Harry.

"It's not that bad," Harry interjects before I can say anything. "Talia just needs to get more prepared."

"Which means she didn't get the loan," Allison confirms while sitting at the kitchen table.

"Bingo," I confirm.

"What did she say you needed to do?" Allison asks.

"Oh, not much," I say carelessly, "just that I need to work in the retail industry for a year to show I know what I'm doing."

"A year?!" Allison screams. "You're living off savings as it is."

"I know!"

"Hold on a minute, guys," Harry says, trying to be the voice of reason, "that was not the only option she proposed to Talia. She did say you needed more experience. But she also said her business plan was shallow and that she could also consider putting someone on her board that has the experience she needs so she could glean the advice from them."

"Yea, Harry, but who do I know that has a successful career in retail?" I complain.

"Be resourceful. This is your dream, right? What are you willing to do for it?" Harry challenges back.

Allison is still taking everything in.

"It sounds like there is a lot that you still need to do to even get this thing off the ground," Allison adds.

"Yes, I have a lot of homework," I confirm.

"What are you going to do?" She asks.

I plop down at the kitchen table with my friend.

"Allison, I don't know."

Allison gets up and hugs me friend from behind the chair.

"You know I'm with you the whole way. I believe in you."

"Yep."

Harry grabs Allison's jacket and they get ready to leave, giving me some time to sort my thoughts.

"We'll talk to tomorrow?" she says.

"Yes, tomorrow."

"Love you, girl."

"I love you too."

WILL TALIA REMAIN DISCOURAGED AFTER HER VISIT TO THE BANK? FIND OUT ON PAGE 149.

"**Give me just five minutes**, Tim. Before I do anything, let me call my fiancée. We just talked about this a couple of days ago and he should be involved in this decision."

Tim just stands in front of my desk, stoic. Then he walks toward my door.

"Very well," he complies.

"Thank you," I reply, running to the door of my office and closing it.

I hesitate before dialing Tony's number. I already know where he stands on this subject. How is this conversation going to go? Part of me just wants to walk back into Tim's' office and tell him that I am walking away.

Just at that moment, the sunlight reflects a prism off my diamond. I look down at my finger and remember the tender moment Tony and I shared when he proposed. I love this man, and if we are going to build a life together, we need to be upfront and honest with each other, no matter the consequences.

I know Tony is only going to be patient for so long. I dial Tony's number, my stomach jittery. My future is on the line.

Tony answers quickly.

"Hey beautiful! How is my fiancée doing?"

"She's feeling a little stressed out and was hoping that you might be able to help."

Tony's tone goes from admiration to concern.

"Of course, sweetheart. What's wrong?"

"I'm still at the office. Been working some long hours on a campaign. I just got cornered by Tim in my office. He wants a decision now. You already know where I stand on this, but I also know that we are on opposite sides of the spectrum. The other night, you told me that you wanted me to be open and honest with you and include you on this decision because it affects both of us. So, I'm calling you."

Tony is quiet at first, taking in all that I've told him.

"Thank you for calling me instead of making a rash decision. I do appreciate that. I know you have been struggling with this for a long time. Ultimately, babe, you've got to make the decision that is going to be best for your family. Forget about me – think about

Jasmine because she's the most important person in this situation. You've done a wonderful job taking care of her and providing a great life for her. If you decide to walk away from this, what does that mean for her? I understand that you are making a sacrifice for yourself to do what you want, but what you have to ask yourself is, will Jasmine be collateral damage in this decision?"

"Tony, I can't believe you're going to guilt trip me about my daughter. You know how much I love her and how much I've sacrificed for her." I am near tears as I start to think about Jasmine and all of that we've been through together.

"Tal, that's exactly why I'm bringing it up. I know how much you love your daughter. I also know your story and what you've been through, moving from your small home town to Atlanta to get your education and get a better job to provide for her. You've done so well for yourself. This offer is a step forward. Do you really want to go backward?"

There is another silence because I am the one thinking now. This doesn't feel like a step backwards to me, but then again, I will be starting over.

"I-I just want to be happy, to live my dream. I'm so tired of feeling so empty," I feel my dream slipping from my grasp.

Tony can feel my emotions over the phone.

"Sweetheart, I'm not asking you to give up your dream. Remember, the decision is still yours to make, but I want you to be aware of the ramifications of jumping into this. You're talking about starting a business that you really don't know a lot about yet. You are starting at the ground floor which does mean you will be taking a step backwards. You will lose a tremendous amount of income and you know that I will do my best to support you and Jasmine, but we're stronger together."

I'm silently weeping now. I wish I wasn't in this position. Tony goes on.

"The other side of the coin is you accept your boss's offer. Do your time. I know that doesn't sound great, but it is what it is. If he is good on his word, he will give you the resources and possibly the capital to start up your store. Even though you must sacrifice working for him a couple more years, isn't that a much better deal?"

I consider Tony's point of view. Logically, it does make sense, and I promised Jasmine that our financial struggles were in the past. This isn't just about me.

"Yes, Tony, I guess you are right. Logically, this does make more sense."

"Just remember what you want. Don't let go of that and it will happen. In the meantime, at least you're getting promoted to partner. That's not a bad deal. Plus, you have me and Jasmine to focus on while you're working there. Focus on us, and the time will fly by."

Life is about sacrifices. I realize that. Maybe this is a sacrifice I need to make to get what I want.

"Okay."

"Call me when it's done."

"Okay."

"I love you."

"I love you, too."

I can do this.

I open my door to find Tim on the other side. Was he eavesdropping?

He extends his hand.

"We have a deal?"

"You were eavesdropping on my conversation?" I ask angrily.

"Not really," he replies nonchalantly, "I had a few things to take care of in my office, then realized how late it was getting so I was heading back to get your decision and could tell you were at the end of your conversation, so decided to just wait. I only heard a few fragments of the conversation since the door was closed. It sounds as if you might be leaning my way," he says expectantly.

I draw in a deep breath as I prepare to satisfy his needs own above my own.

"I guess you heard right," I reply, "but before we move forward with anything, I do want to be certain about one thing."

"What's that?"

"That you make good on your promise to help me start my business. This is important to me and I have no intention of giving up on it."

"And you shouldn't," he says placing his arm around me, "you have my word, and if there's anything I'm good for it's my word. I'll have your contract ready for you to sign in the morning."

⁂

Five years go by quickly. Tony and I have a quick engagement. With the new partnership at the agency, Tim enforced his demands on me immediately. I made plans to start doing marketing research on my boutique during this period so that I would be prepared for the launch when the time came, but I've just been so busy. Tony and I got married. The wedding was beautiful, and Jasmine made an adorable flower girl. At Tim's insistence, we took a honeymoon because he had some aggressive travel plans ahead for me and wanted to make sure I was well rested.

We enjoyed two whole weeks in Hawaii, paradise on earth. It was so nice to finally have some downtime and spend time with my new husband, but unfortunately, that was the last time I remember having any significant downtime. Four years later and I'm still running 100 miles a minute.

Tony and I had a baby a few months ago, and I love being a new mama again. And, Jasmine loves being a big sister. The problem is, I never really had any time to nest and bond with her like I wanted. I worked up to 2 weeks before delivery. I did take 6 weeks off for maternity leave, but I don't know if that would qualify as time off. I still found myself answering emails and putting out fires daily, tainting the time I was supposed to be spending bonding with my new baby girl.

Because of our busy schedules, we had to hire a nanny, and it feels like she spends more time with our girls than we do. Tony was promoted to partner at his firm too, so many times, we are like passing ships in the night barely seeing each other. Jasmine is growing up before my eyes. I feel like I'm missing so much. She's in a soccer league now, and if I'm lucky, I can make one or two games a season.

I'm a slave to my work. Is it this partnership worth it? I have taken on way more than I bargained for and Tim and I have only had fragments of conversations about my boutique in the last five years. Every time I bring it up, he tells me that things are way too busy right now, but we'll discuss it next week, next month, next quarter, next year.

While working late in the office one evening, I come across my old contract that I signed with Tim five years ago. Nowhere in the contract are there any stipulations that state he will help me start my business.

I'm in trouble.

I guess I got screwed!

YEP! THE END.

I sit at the kitchen table and bury my head in my hands. What am I doing? Did I make a mistake leaving my job to pursue this so-called dream of mine? There is so much to sort out and at this point the risk is huge. I look in the living room at my little girl, my heart. Every decision I make will affect her. At this point, I'm wondering if the risk is greater than the reward.

I can stress out about my next steps tomorrow. For now, it is nighttime cuddles with Jazz while we watch her favorite movies.

"Pizza and a movie?"

Jasmine jumps off the couch into my arms.

"Yes, Mommy, yes."

Yep, this is just the therapy I need right now.

It's Saturday and I am not scheduled to work at the boutique today, giving me the full day to spend with Jasmine. I smile, thinking about pizza night with Jasmine last night, then I remember the dreaded bank trip. How are we going to live off savings for the next year? The bank visit yesterday was a big letdown. I felt so optimistic going into the appointment, ready to begin my journey as a boutique owner. And in a matter of minutes, the stiff Ms. Lawson just took it all away.

What if I've bitten off more than I can chew? Tim offered me the chance to start my business with his funding. Why didn't I take it? Is it too late to go back and grovel?

Coffee will help me think more clearly. I head for the stairs, but first peek into Jasmine's room. She is still sleeping. We did stay up late last night.

As the coffee is brewing, I glance at the clock. 9:30.

The day is young. I grab my coffee and get ready to savor my first sip when I hear an unexpected knock at the door. I walk cautiously to the door.

"Who is it?" I say quietly, trying not to wake Jasmine.

"Me," a familiar voice answers, "open the door, girl!"

It's Allison. I open the door, giving my friend a curious expression. She rarely shows up unannounced.

"I come bearing gifts," she says, hands full of bags from our favorite breakfast spot.

"What are you doing here this early?"

"First of all, it's not that early," Allison says, "it's nearly 10:00. I knew you needed some girl time this morning. You looked so dejected yesterday after the bank visit, and while I love Harry, he doesn't see things quite like you and I sometimes. He's more of a black and white guy. So, let's talk. Is Jasmine up? I brought her favorite."

I look upstairs, just in case we woke her, but it is still quiet.

"No, she's still sleeping. We stayed up late last night watching movies and eating junk food."

"Good. Let her sleep, then we can talk," Allison places a comforting hand on mine. "But, first, let's eat. Dig in."

We start to eat our favorite breakfast sandwiches. Sun dried tomato bagel with egg, spinach and cheese. Yum! Comfort food.

Once we've gotten some food in our bellies, Allison looks at me seriously.

"Okay, Tal, what are you thinking?"

"What do you mean?"

"I know you well. You're evaluating your options after yesterday. What are you thinking about doing?"

I feel conflicted.

"I don't know, Allison. Honestly, I'm wondering if I made a mistake leaving the agency. I'm wondering if I should beg for my old job back."

"Wow!" Allison says.

"What?"

"I knew yesterday rocked you, Tal, but I've never taken you for a quitter."

"A quitter?" That stings. "I'm not a quitter."

"No?" Allison challenges, "then why are you ready to give up with the first obstacle you've faced. Look, we've talked about this. This road was not destined to be an easy one, and honestly, pursuing your dreams is never easy. You know that. Even on your road to becoming a creative director at the agency, you had to start at the bottom and work your way up. But you were determined to be successful. You fought and clawed your way to the top, and you made it. Where is that fight in you, Tal?"

I lean back in my chair, reminiscing over that time in my life when I was willing to break down doors to be successful.

"I don't know. Things seem so different now. Back then, my whole motivation was building a solid life for my daughter."

"Isn't that still important to you?"

"Of course, it is. Maybe that's why I feel myself backpedaling. This dream of mine is selfish. The sacrifices I'm willing to make affect my daughter. I can't afford to make her pay for my selfish ambition. That's not fair to her."

Allison understands my trepidation.

"Okay, I get that, but aren't you trying to build a legacy for Jasmine? You can't do that working for the agency. Yes, it is good money, but in the end it's not yours and you don't love it the same. And, the crazy hours will take you away from Jasmine. Build something significant that you can leave to Jasmine, something she can be proud of. Jasmine is a child, but even she understands this is something you need to do."

I shake my head.

"I just don't know how, Allison. I'm scared. Yes, Ms. Lawson did tell me things to do to get started so that I can get the funding I need, but how are Jasmine and I going to stay afloat? I'm so afraid of becoming a failure and landing flat. I have a child to think of. I don't care if I end up on the street, but I'll be damned if I'll put my daughter through that."

"Honey," Allison says, putting her arm around me, "you're thinking of the worst-case scenario. You are not going to end of homeless. Don't even think like that."

I stand up, frustrated, running my hands through my messy morning hair.

"That is a very real possibility if I don't bring in some income while I work on getting this shop up and running," I'm starting to feel a bit desperate.

"Okay, so find a way to make some income. You're resourceful. Work more hours at the boutique. Uber a few hours a week. Do what you must do to accomplish your goals. Stop sounding so defeated."

"I can't help it!" I scream back at my friend, "I'm scared."

Allison walks across the room to me.

"That's perfectly normal. You're taking big, calculated risks. No one does that without facing some fear."

"I don't know how to move past it."

"Mommy," a child's voice interrupts our conversation.

I immediately change my tone. Jasmine can hear the tension in my voice. She looks concerned.

"Good morning baby," I say, giving her a kiss on the cheek, "did you sleep good?"

She nods.

"Mommy, are you okay?"

"Of course, sweetie. Why?"

"You looked worried," she says.

"I'm okay," I say, nonchalantly, "look what Aunt Allison did. She brought your favorite breakfast." I take out Jasmine's breakfast sandwich and immediately her eyes light up.

"Yeah!"

"What do we say to Aunt Allison?"

"Thank you, Aunt Allison!" Jasmine says, runs over to Allison and gives her a big hug.

"Oh, you're welcome sweetheart," she says, returning the love.

"Okay baby, take your breakfast in the living room and watch your favorite cartoons."

"Okay," Jasmine says as she takes her breakfast and starts heading toward the living room, but first she stops short. "Are you guys talking about the clothing store you want to open, Mommy?"

I feel my emotions going into overdrive.

"Go eat your breakfast, Jasmine," Allison directs.

"Okay," she obeys. "Don't worry, Mommy. It's going to be awesome. That's what I tell all my friends at school." Then she disappears into the living room.

"Out of the mouth of babes," Allison says. "Does that change at all the way you're looking at things right now?"

"She is wise beyond her years, that's for sure. But she's a child. She doesn't understand how much it takes to try and do this."

"Then show her, "Allison encourages, "Be an example for your daughter. Show her that when you fall down, you get back up. Yes, this is scary, but you need to be courageous. Having courage means pushing through the wall of fear. You already know how to do this. You've done it. You just need to do it again."

"Yes, I do."

"I'm going to leave you to do that," Allison offers. "I know what I want for you. You deserve to go after your dreams and do what you've always wanted to do, but I can't tell you what to do. Ultimately, you've got to make the decision for yourself. Just know that no matter what, I will always love and support you."

"I appreciate that, Allison."

I walk my friend to the door and give her a long hug.

"I don't want to let you down," I say.

"Don't let yourself down," she says.

I close the door and ponder Allison's last words, "don't let yourself down." I do want to pursue my dream. There are just so many moving parts. It's just so hard. Is it worth it?

I look at my daughter as she watches her favorite cartoons with a smile on her face.

"It's worth it."

I enjoy a nice weekend with my daughter, and now a new week has begun. I get Jasmine ready for school while preparing for another day at the boutique. Today, I am going to ask Julie, the owner, if there is room for in the schedule to work full-time. That will give me a little more breathing room moving forward, even though the pay is laughable compared to my salary at the agency.

During my first break, I ask Julie if I could speak with her. Julie knows about my goal to open a shop of my own and is very supportive.

"How are things going with your new shop, Talia?" Julie asks.

"Not as optimistic as I'd hoped. It's a bit delayed for now. The bank wants me to have more experience to prove that I can run a shop successfully. I also need to work on my business plan. So, it appears I still have a long way to go."

Julie places a comforting hand on my back.

"Don't get discouraged. The process isn't easy. You're going to face roadblocks along the way. Lord knows I sure did."

"Really?" For some reason, this surprises me. Julie is so strong, and her business is thriving. "But, you're so successful now."

"Yes," Julie says, "but I've been in business for seven years and there have been multiple times that I wanted to throw in the towel and quit. It's not an easy business. I won't sugar coat it for you. If it is truly what you want to do, it's worth it. If it's any consolation to you, it took me two years to open up my shop from the time I decided I wanted to do it."

Two years?! I don't have the time or patience to give two years before getting started. I've already given up so much. Julie reads into my silence.

"Hang in there. One baby step at a time," she starts to walk away.

"Julie," I call out to her, "is there any way I might be able to increase my hours here at the shop? I could really use the experience."

Julie pauses for a moment, thinking.

"Are you interested in full-time?"

"Yes."

"I think I might be able to accommodate you. I have someone who is leaving in the next two weeks and I need to cover her hours. I can't do 40 hours but could maybe get you 30-35 hours. Would that help?"

"Yes, it would," I say.

I start to walk back on the floor, when Julia stops me.

"Why don't you go ahead and take the rest of the day off? You only have a couple hours left in your shift and it is kind of slow right now. Plus, you'll be picking up more hours in the next couple of weeks, so we'll make up for it."

"Okay," I say, thankful to have the time to think. I feel so overwhelmed.

I feel my phone buzz as I walk out of the shop.
TONY.

We haven't spoken in weeks. Why is he calling now? I hesitate, wondering if I should even pick up. Our breakup was so painful, and my wounds have not fully healed. I still love him. The phone keeps buzzing. I can't ignore him forever. I decide to bite the bullet.

"Hello."

"Oh hi," Tony says, "I almost hung up. I thought I'd missed you. Or maybe that you just didn't want to talk to me."

"Tony, you know I always like talking to you. It's just that we don't seem to see eye to eye these days, so there's not much to say."

"I miss you."

"Tony, don't say that."

"Why? I do."

"I know, but I just don't see how we can be together now. We don't want the same things. It's best to cut the cord so we stop hurting each other."

"I don't believe that for one second, Talia. I love you, and when you love someone, you fight for them. We may not agree on some of your latest decisions, but it doesn't mean we can't come together and figure it out. Don't we at least owe it to each other to try?"

My mood softens. He has a point. It certainly would be easier to navigate through my hurdles with Tony on my side. I need him. Is he willing to change his perspective and support me?

"I guess you're right."

"Are you willing to give me another chance?" he asks boldly.

There's silence on the line.

"Talia?"

"Yes."

"Yes, you're willing to give us another chance?"

"Tony, I…" I'm flustered.

"What about this? Have dinner with me. We can discuss it then. I want to see you, Talia."

What harm can there be in a simple dinner?

"Okay."

"Tomorrow night? 6:00?"

"Okay."

"I can't wait to see you."

I hang up the phone, hopeful that I may gain an ally in my struggle to chase my dream. But, in my heart, I just don't know.

I look in the mirror while putting the finishing touches on my makeup, anticipating my dinner with Tony. Allison comes over to watch Jasmine.

"Wow, hot mama," she chants as I make my way down the stairs.

"Is it too much?" I say, turning around for my friend in my favorite red V-neck mini dress, "I don't want to appear anxious."

"Are you?" Allison asks inquisitively.

"No," I say sounding uncertain, "I-I don't know. I do still love him. That doesn't just go away. I'm just not sure we can make it work."

"Why are you having dinner with him?" Allison plays devil's advocate.

"Because I saw something in his eyes, something that made me believe that he was willing to see things differently this time. He wants another chance. I can't say that I'm ready to give him that, but I'm willing to at least hear him out."

Allison walks over to me.

"I think that's fair," she says, straightening out a loose curl in my hair, "just remember what's important to you. It's okay that you love him. I like Tony, but don't compromise what's important to you to try and please him. That's why you broke up, remember? If you decide to be couple again, it's important that you work together. You need someone who is going to support you right now, not someone who is going to constantly criticize what you're doing."

"I know, Allison. You're right."

"Don't forget."

"I won't."

"Other than that, try to have some fun. There's been a lot going on these last few weeks. You need to have a little fun, let your hair down a bit. It might be a good thing to spend some time with Tony."

"I'm hoping so," I say, clutching my purse. "Don't wait up."

As I walk into the restaurant, things feel strangely awkward, like it's our first date. So much has happened in the last few weeks, and I'm not sure how to approach this situation, how to approach him.

I spot him and walk toward his table. Tony is a gentleman as always.

"You look beautiful," he leans over and kisses my cheek.

Then, he pulls my chair out and waits for me to sit before sitting down himself.

"It's good to see you," he smiles.

"It's good to see you too," my cheeks flush crimson.

"How have you been?"

"Pretty good, I guess."

"You guess?" Tony prods.

I'm not ready to reveal my latest challenges to Tony yet, not knowing if he is willing to take my side and support me.

"I mean each day is an adventure. I'm learning new things and the process of going into business for yourself is hardly as predictable as working at the agency. It's quite exciting."

"I see," Tony is processing every word.

"What about you?" I am anxious to change the subject. "How are things at your job?"

Tony relaxes a bit.

"Busy," he says, "but I'm loving being junior partner. I'm learning so much more about how the business is run and what makes it tick. It's another challenge and you know I love a challenge. The only downside is that it definitely comes with longer hours and a higher level of dedication, but I'm handling it."

"Good, that's really good. I'm happy for you."

"You know, you could have that too, if you wanted, a partnership."

A cold chill travels up my spine.

"Yes Tony, I know, but that's not what I want, and you know that. Why did you ask me to dinner tonight?"

"I thought you already knew," he reaches across the table to take my hand. "I told you already. I miss you. I don't feel like we took the time to work through our issues before you just walked away. I never wanted us to end. Talia, I love you."

I hesitate before saying anything. I love him too. The warmth of his hand around mine feels good, familiar.

"Do you still love me?"

"Of course, I do," I don't hesitate to answer, "but a relationship needs more than love to survive, I told you that already."

"Love is always enough."

I slowly pull my hand away.

"No, it isn't," I'm unwavering. "If it was enough, more couples would stay together. There would be a lot less divorces in the world. It's just not that simple. I wish it was, but it's not. A relationship requires love yes, but also support, respect and understanding."

"I thought we had all of that," Tony frowns.

"We did," I fidget with the white napkin in my lap, "until I changed the game on you. You like things organized in a neat little box, and I can respect that about you. I know that it was not easy for you to process why I'd turn down the partnership offer to go off into the unknown and pursue my dream. I didn't necessarily expect you to jump onboard immediately. It was a huge risk, I know…"

Tony interrupts me.

"Huge and incredibly reckless."

I lean back in my chair and just close my eyes. Here we go again.

"This was a mistake," I rise from my chair, "I should have never agreed to this."

Tony grabs my arm.

"That's it?" he asks, "we haven't even had dinner yet."

Tears are forming beneath my eyelids.

"I don't know why I thought you'd changed," I say, "but I was open to the possibility that we might be able to get on the same page."

Tony's grip softens.

"Don't give up on me just yet."

I hesitate.

"Please," he pleads, "Stay. Have dinner with me."

I slowly lower myself back into my chair.

"Okay," I say hesitantly, "but anymore comments like that and I'm gone. I mean it."

"I know you do," he chuckles. "You are probably the most headstrong person I know."

"It's served me well."

The mood at the table lightens and we begin to feel more comfortable with each other, like old times. We steer away from conversations about my business decisions for a while and just enjoy dinner together.

After about an hour, things are going so well, so we decide to order dessert.

"I've enjoyed this evening together, Tony. I'm glad I stayed."

"I'm glad you did, too," he says affectionately as he holds my hand across the table.

Though I am enjoying this tender moment with Tony, the fact remains that our relationship has a major conflict. How can I move forward with him when he doesn't support my dreams?

"Tony?"

"Yes…"

"I think it's time to address the elephant in the room. We can't just keep skirting around the very thing that broke us apart in the first place. I need to know if there is a way for us to find our way back to each other."

"Do you love me?" he asks.

"Yes."

"Then, there is always a way."

"That's so much easier said than done. Do you understand why I walked away in the first place? Do you know how I felt?"

Tony pauses, scratching his temple.

"Yes and no," he says.

"Explain."

"I'm a practical guy, you know that. I see everything in black and white, like you said. The stuff in between can be difficult for me to grasp. I understand that you have a dream to open this boutique, and while it is a risky venture, I do support it. I don't want you to think I don't. All I want is for you to be happy. I also want to see you successful and I don't want to see you struggle. The practical side of me couldn't understand why you feel the need to give up everything you've worked so hard to build, a stable life for you and your daughter, to go all-in on something you barely know anything about. That's what I'm struggling with."

I try to understand Tony's point of view. His concerns are valid and make sense, and in his world, my decision to give up everything probably does seem insane. I try to think of the best way to articulate my feelings in a way that he will understand.

"You're right. I took an incredible risk, and I understand how that can be a red flag for you. The best way for me to explain is that I led from my heart instead of my head, and I know that's not your usual protocol. I was feeling suffocated at the agency. I know the opportunity I was offered was incredible, but that is not my future. Not anymore. Even if I were to look at it as a temporary fix, I was afraid I would get lost in the responsibilities of becoming partner and lose my dream. It's what happens to so many people. I'm sorry if I disappointed you by making a decision you wouldn't make yourself, but I felt attacked when I really needed you. That's why I walked away. I can't be around anyone that cannot support me right now because I'm scared and vulnerable."

Tony walks over and wraps me in his strong arms.

"Come on, let's go."

He pays the check, and we walk out of the restaurant.

"Let's take a walk," he says.

We walk in silence for a while. It's nice.

We stop and sit on a nearby bench.

"You don't have to be alone in this, Talia. I want to support you."

"But…"

"No buts, I love you and want to be here for you. If you're scared, I want help you not to be. But you need to be honest and upfront me with. Can you do that?"

"Yes."

"Okay, how are you doing right now?"

I am afraid to confess the challenges in my life right now, but if we are going to try to repair our relationship, I need to be honest about my feelings.

"I'm frazzled, Tony."

"Why?"

"I went to the bank to get a business loan a little while ago."

"And?"

"And I was denied. The loan officer told me what I needed to do but it may take me a year to get where I need to be, just to get financing. I just don't know how I can keep myself afloat until then."

Tony rubs my back affectionately.

"It's going to be okay. We'll figure something out. Can I maybe suggest something if you're willing to keep an open mind?"

"What's that?"

"This may not be the most popular choice for you right now, but just bear with me. What if you go back to your old boss and see if you can get your job back?"

"What?!"

"I know that's not the road you want to go down long-term, but didn't he offer to help fund your business and introduce you to key players in the industry if you were willing to work with him as partner for a few years?"

"Yes but…"

"Look, I'm not saying that he may still have that offer on the table for you, but isn't it worth it to see if he might still be willing to work with you? It's not what you want to do, I know, but it could be exactly what you need right now. You may have to wait at least a year to get the funding you need from the bank, but in the meantime, this can prevent you from hemorrhaging financially."

I think about Tony's suggestion. It does make sense from a practical point of view, but what will I be compromising in the process?

"I-I just don't know, Tony."

Tony threads his fingers with mine.

"Look, I don't want to pressure you. I just don't like to see you stressed. I know that you want to build this business and go after your dreams and I really admire you for that, even if I don't show it. I also know that you want to build a future and a legacy for Jasmine. It is a blow to your ego to go back to your old boss and I know it is not something you want to do, but if you still get the result you want, does it really matter how you get there?"

Tony has a point.

"I guess you're right."

"It's at least worth a shot, right, and if he doesn't take you back, we'll figure something else out. The goal is to help you stay afloat while you build your business. Let's figure out the best way to do that. Who knows? Maybe he'll agree to let you come back part-time which will give you more time to do what you need to do."

"That's true. I guess it won't hurt to try, even though it will be a supreme blow to my ego."

"But worth the peace of mind in knowing your finances are taken care of, right?"

"Yeah, I guess."

"Plus, won't the income you make at the agency help you put more money aside for the business? If you have to wait at least a year before you would qualify to get funding to start your boutique, let's make the best of that year. Let's get prepared."

"Okay."

"Are we still good?"

"Of course, we are still good."

"Can I be your boyfriend again?"

I admire Tony's courage to be open about his feelings and I appreciate that he is trying his best to be supportive, even if his first suggestion is to go back to work for Tim.

"Yes, you can," I give him a hug and a gentle kiss.

"Actually, I want to be more than your boyfriend," he reaches into his pocket.

"Remember this?" he opens a little box that reveals the engagement ring he'd placed on my finger months ago.

"Yes, I do."

"I know we've been through a lot of ups and downs these last few months, but if there's anything I'm sure of Talia Cooper, it's that I love you and want to spend the rest of my life with you. Will you be my wife? And if you say yes, this time, you have to agree to put this ring on your finger and never take it off. We can work though anything - together."

I stare at the beautiful ring, tearing up again. I vividly remember the moment when Tony proposed the first time. I need a partner who will support me through all my ups and downs, but I don't want to be presumptuous.

"Tony, you know I love you," I close the box gently, "but let's take things slow. I want to be your wife, but, let's get our relationship back on track before we start talking about marriage again."

I see the disappointment in Tony's face. I hate letting him down.

I caress his face in my hands.

"I'm not saying no – just right now. Hold onto that box for me and keep it safe."

Tony forces a smile.

"I love you," I reassure him.

"I know you do," he says, "and I love you, too. I'm willing to wait because you're worth it."

"Yes, I am," I smile.

"It's getting late. We should probably head back."

We walk back to the restaurant toward our cars, holding hands the entire way. The walk back is silent just like before, but I have a renewed confidence. Things are going to work out this time. Now, to deal with a whole new problem– Tim Stevens.

HAS TONY CONVINCED TALIA TO BEG FOR HER JOB BACK? TURN TO THE NEXT PAGE.

Sweat beads across my forehead as I make the trek to an old, familiar place. As I roll into the agency parking lot, my phone buzzes.

It's Allison.

"Are you sure you want to do this?"

"I don't know, Allison."

"You don't have to, you know. You shouldn't feel pressured to ask for your job back just because of Tony."

I hesitate.

"I don't even know if I'm doing it just because of him. Yes, he brought it up, but he didn't pressure me to do this. He just wanted me to be less stressed, and let's face it, I'm stressed."

"This isn't what you want, Talia."

"I know, but it might have to be a means to an end. I have more than myself to consider and I cannot afford for me and Jasmine to be living on the streets."

"I told you that would never happen."

"Maybe not, but I have to consider all possibilities. I'm not saying that I will take this job and who knows, Tim may not even want me back, but I've got to try. One of the things he offered me when I talked to him about my business venture initially was funding and mentorship. He's very successful. As much as I hate to admit it, I need his help."

"Yeah, but at what cost?"

"That's what I'm here to find out."

"You know I wish you the best of luck. I just want you to be happy and I know that working here doesn't make you happy anymore."

"I promise to keep my mind focused on the goal at hand. I won't lose sight of that."

"You better not. Good luck. Sorry I can't be there as moral support. They have me at a client site today."

"It's okay. I feel your support in spirit. I'll call you as soon as we're done."

"You better," Allison says before hanging up.

I debate whether I am ready come back to this place. There is only one way to find out. I have to walk in.

I approach Tim's secretary and, she greets me with a big smile.

"What a pleasant surprise seeing you, Talia! Are you here to see Mr. Stevens?"

"Yes, I am."

Hearing my voice outside his office, Tim approaches me with a wry smile on his face.

"Well, look what the cat dragged in. Good to see you, Talia. Come on in."

I walk slowly into my old boss's office, nervous about the outcome of this meeting. What if he says no? Will I be disappointed or relieved? What if he says yes? Will it be a win or a loss? Suddenly, my clear objective for this meeting becomes muddled. I don't know what I want. I feel like running but that is no longer an option.

Sensing my hesitation, Tim motions toward the chair in front of his desk.

"I won't bite. Have a seat."

I sit cautiously.

"How's life as a business owner? You were starting a clothing boutique, right?"

I fidget nervously. I want to appear confident, but I am failing miserably.

"It's coming along, just not quite as swiftly as I'd hoped."

Tim leans back in his chair, smiling. He's such a prick.

"Well, owning a business is not all it's cracked up to be. It takes hard work and dedication. It's your baby and it needs to be fed. My assistant, Dawn, told me that she saw you working at one of the boutiques downtown, is that true?"

This is embarrassing.

"Yes, I'm only there part-time. My loan officer suggested that I get some real-world experience in retail or bring someone on my board of directors that has years of experience. I figured this had to be a start."

"So, I take it the bank did not give you a loan?" Tim rubs his chin pensively.

Saying it out loud makes me feel like such a failure, especially in front of him.

"No," I bow my head in contrition. I hate that I've been reduced to this. "I may have bitten off more than I can chew. I want to do this, and I do believe I will be successful, but the bank doesn't hand out loans on just ambition alone."

"No, it doesn't," Tim stares at me deadpan.

An awkward silence falls over the room. It is as if we both know why I am here and each of us is too stubborn to make the first move.

Getting up, I think to leave while I still have a shred of dignity.

"Talia, why did you come here today?"

I slowly sink back into my chair, seeing no way out. I have to let go of my pride.

"I was just wondering…. well…if you…if you'd…"

"If I what?"

He's toying with me. He wants me to say it.

"If my old job was still available."

There. I've spit it out. There is no back pedaling now.

Tim leans back in his chair, a self-gratifying smile crawling across his face. He has me right where he wants me. He sees the defeated look in my eyes. He knows how hard this is for me.

"Your old job? You mean your creative director position?"

I nod.

He looks intently into my eyes.

"I'm sorry, Talia, that job is not available."

I don't know why I've come here anyway. Perhaps this is a blessing in disguise.

"But," he said, "I still need a partner and my partner will have to absorb the creative director position for a little while until we find an adequate replacement. I used to have a kick-ass creative director, but she decided to leave to pursue her own business. Whoever takes on this position needs to be dedicated to the agency. Fully dedicated. Do you know anyone who can fill this role for me?"

I know what Tim is asking of me even though he has not officially offered me the job. He wants my full, undivided attention, which means if this position is available, I'll have to give up the dream I've become so attached to. Am I ready to do that?

"I might know someone," I reply softly.

"You might, or you do?" Tim prompts.

He wants an answer and is not going to back down until I give him one.

"I have some questions," I say.

Tim's expression grows defiant.

"I think you've lost the right to ask me anything. You do realize I don't have to offer you anything?"

Asshole!

That's my cue. I'm leaving. I rise from my chair.

"Sit down." It's a command not a request.

I slide back into my chair. This was a bad idea.

"Talia, why are you here?"

I am humbled, sitting here in Tim's office, considering his old offer.

"Because I'm stuck," I blurt out, "I thought I could do this and now I'm not so sure. I need help."

Tim leans over his broad mahogany desk. I've intrigued him.

"And you think I can help you?"

I nod.

"That is – if you're willing to."

"Good point, Ms. Cooper. I do need to be willing. I must ask because I'm a businessman and I do believe in getting a return on my investment. Why would I help you?"

I swallow hard. I don't know how to answer his question.

"I was hoping you could help me figure this out."

Tim laughs. It's a sarcastic laugh.

"You want me to help you figure out how to start your own business. That's rather counterintuitive, isn't it?"

"You offered to help me before," I remind him.

Tim picks up a trinket off his desk and begins toying with it.

"That was then. This is now."

"So, you don't want to help me?" I ask.

"That depends."

"Depends on what?"

"It depends on what you're willing to do for me. Life doesn't come in a neat little package. You've lost the privilege of making demands. You came crawling back to me which means I hold all the cards. What I offer you take, or you can get the hell out of my office."

"Yes, but…"

"No buts, Talia. I've lost my patience with you. "

I'm livid but I maintain my control. I did come back to him after all.

"What are your terms?"

"I bring you on as my partner and nothing else," he says, "I will help with your business on my terms and when I'm ready. And I say now I'm not ready. My priority is growing this agency and if you join as my partner, that will be your priority as well. If I suspect even an inkling of you doing something else, I'll fire you so fast, it will make your head spin. That's my offer."

I don't want this. I'd be coming back to a prison.

"You have a daughter, don't you?" Tim reminds me.

I nod.

"Think about her."

Bastard. Why did he have to bring Jasmine into this? But he's right. She does need stability.

"Can I have some time to think on this?"

Tim throws his hands in the air.

"Of course, you do. Don't you always?" he seethes.

I'm silent.

"You have 24 hours, and then I'm rescinding the offer."

I sit there frozen, as Tim weaves through the papers on his desk.

"You can see yourself out," he doesn't even look up.

I feel nothing but contempt for this man. Why would I want to come back and work for him?

Riding home, I feel angry and desperate at the same time. I've never seen Tim like this. What would it be like if I come back to work for him? I sense he'll keep me on a short leash. Am I willing to sacrifice a few years to work at the agency to capitalize on Tim's expertise, expertise that he seems reluctant to give me? Will he even help me? His attitude was cynical and self-serving today. I can't be sure he's even willing to help me anymore. What if he does? That would be a game changer. I need a warm bath followed by a hot cup of coffee before I deal with all of this.

The bath calms my mind and body from the stress of the day. I bask in the solitude of my home since Jasmine is spending the night with a friend. Is it crazy to even think about turning Tim down - again? Or, is it crazy to take his pity offer? What is my backup plan? How am I going to start this boutique?

The doorbell interrupts my concentration.

I open the door. Tony stands there smiling sheepishly.

"I'm sorry. I should have called first. I just took a chance that maybe I could catch you at home. Did you meet with your old boss?"

I am relieved to see Tony. I am hoping he'll be a sounding board.

"Yes, I did," I say, swinging the door open to let him in.

I walk back to the kitchen table to nurse my cup of coffee.

Tony pulls up a chair, looking at me expectantly.

"Well?"

I roll my eyes, recounting the events of our meeting.

"It was not a fun meeting, but he did make an offer."

"Was it as good as the first offer?" Tony leans forward.

"He put the partnership back on the table."

"He did?" Tony says, surprised, "that's huge, Talia!"

"Is it, Tony? Tim was a complete ass. He berated me the entire time I was in his office. He knows that I need him, and he's enjoying every minute of it "

Tony wraps his arms around me.

"I'm sorry baby, but let's put feelings aside for a minute. Going back to the agency will help restore your finances while you try and figure some things out. It will help alleviate the stress you're feeling."

I break away from Tony and start pacing the floor.

"I'm not so sure, Tony," I'm wagging my finger in the air, "Working for that man might cause me more stress than I'm feeling right now. He told me on no uncertain terms would I be allowed to pursue my dream of opening my store while working for him or he'd fire my ass. How is this moving me forward? I'm not even sure he'll help me. He was very ambiguous about that."

Tony scratches his head.

"Okay, this is not ideal. Maybe you just need to regain his trust. You have turned him down already."

I'm getting angry. It feels like Tony is taking his side.

"I don't care about his damn trust, Tony. He showed me no respect. How the hell can I work in an environment like that?"

"Talia, I know you're strong-willed. It's one of the things I love about you. Your stubbornness can cloud your judgment sometimes. You don't have to like Tim, but you can capitalize on what he has to offer. It's business. Take your feelings out of this."

"I can't!" I scream. "My feelings are wrapped all up in this. I've been operating off intuition since I decided to go down this path."

"Maybe that's the problem," Tony chimes in.

"Really?"

"Your intuition doesn't always call on your logic to make the best decisions."

"All decisions aren't made on logic, Tony."

"Give me one example," he challenges.

"My relationship with you," I fire back, "I'm not with you out of logic. Love doesn't always make sense. I followed my heart when I fell in love with you which had nothing to do with logic, but right now, at this moment, my intuition is telling me that I was right to break up with you the first time."

"Wow," Tony says, turning to put his coat on, "you're upset and saying things you don't really mean right now. I'm going to leave so that you can calm down. If you want to discuss this further, call me."

He leaves, no good-bye, no hug, no kiss – nothing. I fear it is a permanent good-bye. I thought he'd had a change of heart, but he's singing the same old song.

Tossing and turning, I can't my brain off. It's an endless night. I hated fighting with Tony. I want to be with him again, but I fear history is repeating itself. I glance at my alarm clock.

2:11 am.

I fall back into the bed, wide awake and exasperated. What now? I look at my phone. There is only one person who might understand what I am feeling right now.

I pick up my phone, pause, then dial his number.

"Talia?"

"Zack, I'm so sorry, did I wake you?"

"I'm awake now, is everything okay? Jasmine, is she…?"

"She's fine," I interrupt, "I need to talk to you."

"At two in the morning?"

"I can't sleep."

Zack chuckles.

"What's so funny?"

"Woman, you're lucky I have a soft spot for you. If we didn't have a child together, I wouldn't have even picked up the phone."

"Wow, it's like that now?"

"We haven't been a couple in a long time. And, you have a fancy boyfriend now, or are you guys still broken up?"

"It's complicated."

"It always is."

"I didn't mean to bother you. It's just… you know me better than anyone. I know we're not together but you're still my best friend."

"Okay, you've buttered me up enough. What you got?"

"You know I want to start this boutique?" I ask.

"Oh yeah, how's that going?"

"Not good."

"Talk to me."

"I got with Allie's boyfriend to run some numbers on the financing I needed. Then, we went to see a loan officer. I was denied. I didn't show them that I was qualified enough to do this and make it successful. Because I don't have a fashion and retail background, they are holding that against me. If I had a business partner with industry experience or at least a year of experience myself, they might reconsider."

"Okay…"

"I'm stuck, Zack."

"Sound like your solution is pretty simple to me."

"Really? Can you share your simple solution with me, because the answer has not been that apparent through my eyes?"

"Your money guy says you need a partner with more experience in the fashion industry? Go find a partner that knows what they're doing. In the meantime, go get some experience yourself. What's the problem?"

"Zack, it's just not that simple. First, where am I going to find a partner? I don't even know where to start. Second, I quit my job and started working at a local boutique to gain some experience. We're living off my savings. I don't know how much longer I can do this. I'm not making enough to make this work – not for a year. So, I made a desperate move."

"Talia, what did you do?"

"I went back to the agency and asked my boss for my old job."

"You didn't?"

"I did."

"You were that desperate?"

"It was Tony's idea, but yea, I guess I was."

"Isn't that why you guys broke up?" He asks.

I sigh.

"Yes."

"Why the hell are you taking his advice now?" Zack is incensed.

"Tony and I reconciled. He's trying to see things from my perspective. We're trying to make it work."

"He's trying to see things from your perspective, yet he convinced you to go back to your old boss and beg for your job?"

It sounds awful when he says it like that.

"Are you going to listen to me or not?"

"Fine," he concedes, "what did your boss have to say?"

"He was so arrogant, Zack! He said everything had to be on his terms, take it or leave it. He gave me the option of partner but told me that I'd have to be 100% committed to working for him and nothing else. And, if I didn't, he'd fire me."

"So pretty much indentured servitude?"

"Yep."

"Is that what you want?"

"Of course not."

"So why is this decision so hard? Why are you losing sleep over this?"

"Zack, I don't know if I have a choice. I don't know how to move forward. Nothing is going the way I envisioned it."

"That's normal, Talia. You're going against the grain so of course; you're going to encounter some challenges. Did you think this would be easy?"

"No, I guess not."

"You give up too easily."

"Who said I was giving up?"

"You just said you were contemplating going back to your old job."

"To secure my finances," I defend. "It's not my long-term solution. If Tim makes good on his promise, at least I can learn what I need to from him and gain his valuable connections."

"At the expense of starting a business of your own," Zack says. "Did he even say how long you'd have to work for him in exchange for this favor he's doing for you?"

"No."

"Well, you need to know that. What if he wants you to work for him ten years before he's willing to help you? Do you want to wait that long? If he's willing to do all these things for you, hold him to it. Make him put it in writing. Otherwise, he may hold it over your head indefinitely and you will be stuck."

"I don't know that he'll do that. He told me that since I've already turned him down, he was essentially doing me a favor. He said I'm not in the position to make demands."

"That's bullshit, Talia. You need to walk."

"And, if I don't take this job, what do I do then?"

"You'll figure it out. If you want to start this boutique like you told me, you are going to have to get your hands a little dirty and be willing to be uncomfortable for a while. It won't be easy, but if it's what you want, and I think you do, you'll figure out how to make it work."

I smile.

"I thought I was the smart one."

Zack laughs.

"I'm not all brawn, but you broke up with me, remember?"

"Yea, I remember. Probably not my smartest decision."

There is a slight pause in our conversation. Zack gets me. I'm not sure Tony does. Maybe I'm with the wrong guy.

"You've made a lot of great decisions, Talia, and you'll figure this out, too. Whatever you decide, I know it will be the best for you and Jasmine. You know you have my full support."

I take a chance.

"Zack?"

"Do you ever think about us?"

"Us?"

"Back in the old days when we were a couple."

He's quiet for a while.

"Sometimes."

"We were good together, right?"

"Yeah, I think so."

"What went wrong?"

"Talia, we were young and trying to figure out a lot of things, like becoming parents. You don't make the best decisions when you're a kid."

"You think it was a bad decision for us to break up?" I ask.

"Talia, I never wanted to break up with you, but I couldn't hold you back either. I had to set you free. Where is all of this coming from?"

"I don't know. I guess I'm feeling nostalgic, wondering what could have been. Anyway, I know it's late. Thanks for talking this out with me."

"At two in the morning."

'Yes, at two in the morning."

"You know I love you if I will talk to you at two in the morning."

"I appreciate you, Zack. Good night."

"Good night, Talia."

Wait, what? Did he just say he loved me?

I relish a quiet morning on a weekday which is a rare occurrence. I rarely allow Jasmine to have sleepovers on a school night, but I need the time to think without distractions.

As I lean over the kitchen counter, enjoying my coffee, my phone buzzes.

"Hello."

"Talia."

It's Tony.

"I hated the way we left things last night."

"It did get a little ugly, didn't it?" I say.

"I didn't mean to upset you."

"It's okay. I tend to get upset quite easily these days. There's a lot going on and I'm finding myself on edge more than usual."

"Did you make a decision?" He presses.

"I'm still working through it but I'm feeling more at peace about it."

"You don't want to tell me, do you?"

"I think this is something I need to figure out for myself. Will my decision make a difference with us?"

"Talia, I love you, and will support whatever you decide to do. I'd like to be a part of your decision, but I understand if you feel like you need to work through this on your own. Just do me one favor?"

"Yes."

"Keep me in the loop. Don't shut me out. Call me and let me know how it goes," he requests.

"Of course."

"I won't try to influence you either way. I know you well enough to know that you're going to do what you want anyway."

I laugh.

"You're right about that."

"You do seem to be in better spirits. Whatever changed, I'm glad for it. I'll talk to you later?"

"Count on it."

I hang up the phone, realizing my career direction isn't the only conflict I'm faced with. My high spirits are attributed to Zack. He talked me off the ledge last night, and I could have sworn he told me that he loved me.

I walk through the familiar agency doors, confident. Tim is not going to shake me today.

Tim's door is open.

He is peering over his glasses at his computer screen.

My presence interrupts his deep concentration.

"Talia, so good to see you again," he says with a much more pleasant tone than yesterday, "please have a seat."

I sit down.

"How are you?"

"I'm doing fine," I respond, confidently.

"I can only assume that since you're here, that you have something to share with me?"

"I do."

"Shall I draw up the paperwork?"

"Just one thing. You're asking me to commit 100% to a partnership with you. If you are willing to help me start my business after my commitment to you, can you put it in writing?"

"Why would I do that?" He frowns.

"You are asking me to give 100% of myself to your business. If I'm willing to do this, can you at least give me that?" I'm asking for your help."

Tim laughs. The arrogance has returned.

"Talia, this is not a contract. I'm in no way obligated to do those things for you. My expectation to have you commit yourself 100% to the business as my partner is what any employer would ask of their employee – even more so on the partner level."

Any move I make now will have to be on faith – faith in myself or faith in him.

"Does your little interrogation mean that you've decided not to take this offer unless I put in writing how long I want you to work for me? I believe I've made it clear; this is my last and final offer. Take it or leave it."

୧ଡ଼

TIM IS A JERK BUT LET'S HOPE HE'S AN HONORABLE JERK. TRUST THAT HE WILL INVEST BACK INTO YOU IF YOU INVEST IN HIM. TURN TO PAGE 192.

TELL TIM TO SUCK IT AND GO AFTER YOUR DREAM TO START YOUR BOUTIQUE. YOU CAN FIND YOUR SUPPORT SOMEWHERE ELSE. TURN TO PAGE 181.

It is a painful reality to learn that Tony does not believe in my dream. I stare at the ring on my finger; but I love him so much. I want to build a life with him. There was never a question about that from the time we met. He is the one.

"Tony, what would you have me do?" I say, sounding defeated.

And he senses it.

Walking over to me, he wipes the tears from my eyes.

"I do believe in you. I think you are the most amazing woman that I've ever known. That's why I want to marry you. I don't think quitting your job was the best decision you could have made, but it's done. Honestly, I don't know if opening a clothing boutique is the right move for you to make right now."

"Tony, this is something that I've always wanted to do," I plead.

"Tal, if it is something that you've always wanted to do, why haven't we talked about it before now?"

I think about his question for a moment. Why haven't I shared this passion with him before?

"I-I don't know," I say, baffled, "I'm only rediscovering it myself."

"All I'm saying is be sure before you jump in with both feet on something. I know you like clothes and shoes. Your closet says that. That doesn't qualify you to be a clothing store owner. You are a kick-ass graphic designer. You were a great creative director. Maybe you just outgrew working with Tim, unless you might want to reconsider his partnership offer. Do you think he might put it back on the table?"

I snatch away from Tony angrily.

"I don't want to go back to work for that weasel."

Conceding, Tony holds his hands up.

"Okay, okay, we'll move on from that. That option is off the table. If you want to start your own business, why don't you do something that you are already good at and have a reputation for?"

"Graphic design?"

"Precisely," Tony agrees, "you could start out freelancing and you could eventually grow it into a firm if you'd like, but I think that's a great and logical move for you. You would have more freedom in your schedule and be able to spend more time with Jasmine and – plan our wedding."

I speculate Tony's suggestions. Like him, they are logical. Working for myself is very attractive. Maybe he is right. My desire to open a clothing boutique could be a fleeting notion. I was getting stagnant with my position there at the agency, but I've always enjoyed graphic design, and I am very good at it. Because of my reputation in the industry, I won't have much trouble building up a book of clients and I already have an impressive portfolio.

"Okay."

"Okay?" Tony replies surprised at my acquiescence.

"As usual, you make a very convincing argument. Starting a freelance graphic design business makes sense. I have the experience and skill set to get it off the ground quickly and I can use some of the money in my savings to help stay afloat while I get established. I could start making money much faster doing this than I would opening a clothing store without the overhead. I'm not even sure how long it would take to get that going."

Proud to finally be getting his point across, Tony stands up, gesturing strongly.

"That's exactly what I was saying. Do what you know. And, who knows? Maybe once you've gotten established and start making good money, we can re-visit the boutique. We can do our research and wouldn't have to compromise our finances to make it happen. This way, there's no risk involved. Now, let's talk wedding dates."

It's been six months since I left the agency. Tony and I decided on a short engagement and got married two months ago. Since we both have money in savings, we fulfilled my dream of having a destination wedding in Jamaica. It was beautiful. The ceremony was simple and small with just our family and closest friends. Best of all, I got to walk down the aisle in a romantic, flowy gown on the most beautiful beach I'd ever seen – barefoot. Allison still teases me that I went barefoot on my wedding day, as many shoes as I have in my closet, but it was absolutely perfect.

Tony moved into the townhouse and sold his condo which was just a one-bedroom bachelor pad. We both agreed that this made the most sense for our needs right now because my townhouse was more than enough room for the three of us. We plan to buy our first house together within the next year. But, for now, we are working on stabilizing my business income while Tony continues to work at his firm as senior architect.

I was nervous about starting my business at first, but like Tony said, it was an easier start because I was operating in my zone of genius.

Business is picking up and I have a few steady clients now. Tony and I project that by the end of the year, I will be close to replacing most of my original salary. I am spending more time with Jasmine which is something I've always longed to do and knew wouldn't have been possible had I taken the partnership at the agency.

As each day passes, I became more confident that Tony and I have moved forward with the right decision.

Two years later…Life is good! Tony was promoted to partner at his firm a year ago, increasing our income significantly. The unfortunate side of this promotion has been his long hours. Our family has grown by one and Jasmine is a big sister to the most precious 8-month-old little girl, Kaley.

After getting out into the marketplace and promoting myself a little bit, my business has been doing extremely well. Work has picked up so much for me lately that I had to hire a part-time assistant to help me stay organized. I'm designing all the time and since things are going so well, I guess I'm doing what I'm supposed to. But, it's strange, lately, I've been feeling a quiet little nudge, like something is missing. I can't put my finger on it exactly, but I don't feel quite as fulfilled as I should be. I have everything. I should be happy, right?

I GUESS YOU'LL HAVE TO BE. THE END.

I **reach across the desk** and shake Tim's hand.

A wide smile spreads across his face; he thinks he's won.

"Thank you, Tim, for your offer. It has given me a tremendous amount of clarity on what I need to do."

With that, I turn around and starting walking toward the door.

"Talia?"

"Yes, sir."

"Should I have Janet prepare your office? When do you want to start?"

"Oh, I'm sorry. I should have been clearer. I'm declining your offer. I'm going to make my business work. Thank you for helping me see that."

I rush out of the office before he can even formulate a response.

Allison snags me on my way out.

"Talia?"

"Hey there!"

"What happened?"

"Walk down with me. Once Tim realizes what just happened, I'm sure I won't be able to step foot back in this building."

"That bad, huh?" Allison giggles as we take the elevator to the lobby.

Once we're out of the building, Allison turns to me.

"What's the scoop? You must have turned him down."

"Damn right," my chest is poked out like a peacock.

"Good for you!"

"I have no idea what the next step is. I don't know what I'm doing, but I'm not giving up. I know this is what I'm supposed to do and it's too early to throw in the towel."

"I'm so glad to hear that. Whatever you need, I'm here. Just ask, I mean it," she scolds.

"Thanks," I say, "I need all the allies I can get right now."

As I'm driving home, I realize that I need to call Tony. I feel so liberated right now, afraid but courageous. Though I don't have a specific plan, I know things are going to be okay. A sense of calm has fallen over me. I hope Tony shares my sentiments.

"Hey sweetheart, how did the meeting go?"

"I think it went quite well," I'm beaming.

"That's great! You sound confident. Did you to take the job?"

"No, not exactly."

"Not exactly? What does that mean?"

"I declined his offer."

The line sounds dead.

"Tony? Are you still there?"

"Yes, I'm still here. I'm just a little surprised, that's all."

"Why are you surprised? You knew where I stood on everything. I never said I was going to take the job."

"I know you never said that. It's just that…"

"It's just what?"

"You were so stressed, Talia. I thought this might fix things, help ease your financial concerns and help you get what you want."

"That's just it, Tony. I'm not so sure I would've gotten what I wanted. Tim has his own agenda to get what he wants, and I don't think at any point, it includes me getting what I want."

"Of course, he does, Talia. He's a business owner. He's not stupid. He's definitely after his own interests. But what we talked about is you taking advantage of what's he's willing to offer to serve your own interests."

"I understand that, but I talked to Zack last night and he suggested that I ask him to put what he was offering me in writing to make sure he'd make good on what he was offering."

"Wait, you spoke to Zack last night?"

I hesitate. He sounds kind of pissed.

"It was kind of late. I couldn't sleep and needed to talk to someone."

"And he was the first person you thought to call?"

"Well, after the way we left things, you weren't the first one on my list."

Tony is jealous.

"Okay, fine, what did your boss say then?" he's seething, "Was he willing to put things in writing?"

"No, he wasn't."

"So, you said no."

"I said no."

"What are you going to do now?"

"I don't know yet. I just know that working with Tim is not my future. I do need income while I figure out how to start my business, and I'll figure it out."

"You realize it's not as easy as simply saying you'll figure it out."

"Actually, Tony it is. It's where every plan begins. You figure out what to do and then you do it. Thank you for your support. You've been a champ."

Then I hang up on him.

How dare he? He claims to be so supportive but changes his tune as soon as my decision doesn't mirror his own. But is that what really changed his tune?

Tony's jealous of Zack. I wonder if I was too hard on Tony. Maybe I should have listened to more of what he had to say.

My thoughts jumped to the conversation with Zack last night. I called him in the middle of the night, and he took my call and walked me through a stressful situation without complaints. Only after talking to him did I feel a sense of calm to move forward. Something else happened last night…he said he loved me!

I pull in front of the townhouse and just sit here for a minute. I'd almost forgotten. He'd said it so nonchalantly. Did he even mean to say it, or did he mean it like telling a sister, 'I love you'? Why do I care so much? There is no time to agonize over my feelings. Not right now. I need to figure out how I'm going to make money and stay afloat.

I walk into my home and look around. It is a beautiful place. I did this. I was so proud the day I'd purchased this place and now I'm wonder I'm going to be able to keep us here.

"Mommy!" Jasmine runs through the door and wraps me in a big hug.

"Hey sweetheart!" Holding her makes all my worries disappear for the moment.

I wave outside and mouth a quick thank you to her friend's parents for looking after her today.

"What would you like for dinner, sweet girl?"

"Pizza!" she yells.

"You always want pizza. Let's try something else."

Jasmine scrunches her face like she's straining her thoughts.

I know I don't want to cook, but I'm going to have to cut back on the take out with my current financial situation hanging in the balance.

"How about chicken fingers?"

"Yea!! Mommy, can I watch cartoons?"

"Did you finish your homework?"

"Yes, I finished before we came here."

"Then yes. I'll call you when dinner is ready."

I'm on my phone trying to find a place that delivers chicken and it rings. It's Zack.

Butterflies flutter in my stomach.

That's new.

"What's the word?"

"Hey Zack."

"Are you going to tell me or what?"

"What?" I am clueless.

"Your meeting? With your old boss? Why you called me at two am last night."

"Oh yeah, I declined his offer."

"Wow! Really? What changed?"

"What do you mean?"

"Last night, you sounded like you were ready to take the job."

"I was seriously considering it, but I took your advice."

"My advice?"

"Yes, I asked him to put what he was offering in writing."

"And?"

"He said no."

"Well, that was definitive."

"Yep, he was very clear. But, now there's just one problem?"

"What's that?"

"I've closed my only back door and now I have to make this work."

"Yes, you do."

"Can you help me?"

"How can I help?"

"I don't know. You've been so supportive during this process and I'm going to need someone to lean on as I learn how to put one foot in front of the other."

"You know I'll do anything for you, Talia. Whatever you need. Actually…"

"Actually what?"

"I've been thinking of moving out that way. I just got a couple of job offers in that area but wanted to talk to you first. I don't want you to feel like I'm infringing."

"Why do you think you'd be infringing?"

"You have your own life now, and I want to be respectful of that. I'd just like to be closer to my daughter when she needs me. I miss her and want to spend more time with her."

My heart skips a beat at the thought of Zack being closer. Jasmine is not the only one who needs him.

"You wouldn't be infringing at all! And, I know Jasmine would love to have you here." I've got to play it cool.

"You're really okay with it?"

"Of course, Zack. It would be easier for us to co-parent with you here. I do agree with that."

"Okay, and maybe with me there, I can help support you more financially if you need it while you're getting your business up and running. Both job offers are pretty lucrative."

"You don't have to do that, Zack."

"I'm offering, Talia, and right now you need all the help you can get, so stop being stubborn."

"Yes sir."

Zack chuckles.

"Okay, well, I have a couple of days to make a decision on the job. I'd be looking at a start date next month, so I'll probably need to come down in a couple of weeks to look for a place."

"You could stay here."

I just blurt it before realizing what I am saying.

"With you? At your house?"

"Well, yeah, it's a pretty big place and it's just me and Jasmine.

We have an extra bedroom, and like you said, I need some financial support. Why don't I just rent you that room and you can help me with my mortgage? And, you can spend time with your daughter every day."

"Well, sounds good to me. I don't know what your boyfriend is going to think about that. I know I wouldn't be too keen on my girlfriend's ex staying in her house."

"Why don't you let me deal with that? Plus, it would only be temporary until I get my finances stabilized."

"Okay – if you say so. I'm not going to turn down any opportunity to spend more time with Jasmine."

"Good. Now, I have to go because I promised Jasmine chicken fingers and you called before I could order it."

"Okay, tell her I love her."

"I will."

"Goodbye."

How is Tony going to handle Zack coming here? He showed some clear signs of jealousy, so I know he's not going to be happy about it. But, it's what's best for me and Jasmine right now. He'll have to understand that.

&.

"Thanks for having lunch with me today," Tony says as he holds my hand across the table at one of our favorite Italian hot spots.

"We've been butting heads a lot lately. We need to get on the same page if we want this thing to work," I assert.

"I couldn't agree with you more."

"Let me start with what's on my mind right now," I begin.

"Shoot."

"Are you jealous of Zack?"

"No, of course not. Why would you say that?"

"The other day when we were talking on the phone, you were clearly unhappy when I told you that Zack and I had talked on the phone before my meeting with Tim."

"I agree, I was a bit unhappy. What boyfriend would be happy to hear that their girlfriend called their ex in the middle of the night because they were stressed and couldn't sleep? Come on now."

"I see your point. Are you still upset?"

"Are you still calling your ex in the middle of the night?"

"No."

"Then no."

"But I do have something to tell you and I'm hoping you won't be too upset about it."

"What are you setting me up for Talia?"

"Zack is moving to Atlanta."

"Okay."

"He wants to be closer to Jasmine, so he can spend more time with her."

"I think that's great."

"Yes, I agree. He's already received a couple of job offers and may be moving here as soon as next month."

"That's pretty soon. I guess he's been considering this for some time then?"

"I guess so. He just told me, so I don't know how long he's been searching for jobs. He didn't want to accept an offer until he talked to me. He wanted to make sure I was okay with it."

"Why would he think you weren't?"

"I think he was just worried about infringing on my life and my privacy. I want him to have a great relationship with his daughter. I'd never discourage that."

"I know you wouldn't. Is that what you think I wouldn't like?"

"Zack told me that he's going to need to find an apartment, but I made a proposition instead. I suggested that he stay at the townhouse with me and Jasmine."

"What?!"

"Tony, calm down."

"I'll calm down as soon as you tell me you're just joking with me."

"I'm not joking."

"What the hell, Talia?"

"Tony, just listen," I try to calm him with a gentle touch, but it doesn't seem to be working, "there's a method to this madness."

"I sure hope so. Was this his idea?"

"Actually no, it was mine."

Tony's eyes look like they're going to bug out of his head.

"Really? Is there something else you're not telling me? Are you two having an affair?"

"What? No...of course not. Why would you think that?"

"Why do you want to live with your ex-boyfriend?"

"I don't want to live with him. I am in a bit of a financial pickle right now as I try to figure out my finances and get my business off the ground. I have an extra bedroom and if he stays with me, he can pay rent to help with the mortgage while spending time with his daughter every day."

"And he'll stay under the same roof – with you."

"Well, yes, but it would just be temporary, until I get on my feet. You clearly have a problem with this. Zack told me that you probably would."

"Good man."

"Okay genius, do you have any suggestions to help me with my situation?"

"Why don't you just let me help you, Talia?"

"That's a lot to ask, Tony."

"A lot to ask of me but not your ex, Zack."

"I'd be charging him rent."

"Okay, move in with me."

"What?"

"Sell your townhouse to Zack or rent it to him and you move in with me."

"Tony, I..."

"Is it such a big step? We've been dating for a while. I proposed to you. You gave me my ring back but I'm hoping to change your mind and put that ring back on your finger. It's a logical next step in our relationship."

"Is that what you want?"

"Talia, I want you."

"Can I think about it?"

"As long as you don't move your ex in before you give me your answer."

"Okay. It's a deal."

"Good. Now, what are we going to do about your situation? You're jobless and don't know how to get your business started. What are you going to do?"

I lean back in my seat, taking a long, deep breath.

"Honestly, Tony, I just don't know. I had a little nest egg in my savings which I wanted to use as seed money to get something started. I've already started eating through some of it."

"I bet about now you probably wish you weren't so presumptuous about quitting your job and starting your business."

"Don't be smug. I don't have any regrets. I just don't have a plan."

"You're right, so you need to come up with something, quick. No matter what your plan is for your business, you need a way to make money. Have you thought of approaching another agency to see if they'd be willing to take you on as a creative director?"

"Tony, I don't want another job. That's not what I'm trying to do right now."

"Whether you want a job or not, you need one. You just told me your savings are dwindling. You barely have enough money to even begin to think of starting a business. The bank won't give you any money and you're running out of money to live on. Your supply is running out and no matter how much support you have, you're going to have to start doing something to make money again soon."

"Why are you trying to stress me out?"

"I'm not trying to stress you out, Talia. I'm a realist. I'm not discouraging you from starting your business. I just want to help you keep your head above water."

I look at Tony sheepishly.

"So, you're saying you're not willing to take care of me?"

His tone softens.

"You know I will, but I know you. That's not what you want. You don't like people taking care of you. You like to hold your own. I want you to be able to do that, but we've got to figure out what that looks like because the reality is your business is not going to start turning profit right away. It will take time, but you have to get started first."

"You're right. I haven't even gotten started. I don't know how."

"That's what you need to figure out. Figure out how to make it work with your limited resources. But, seriously, honey, you need a job."

He's right. I am spinning my wheels.

"Any suggestions?"

"The firm just announced that they are looking for a marketing director. With your background, I'm sure you'd be a done deal."

"Full-time?"

"Yes."

"Do you think there will be room for me to run my business and get things off the ground and do that job too?"

"It's possible. It's a demanding position, I'm not going to lie to you. You'd be responsible for managing the marketing for the entire company. You'd have your own team and you'd probably have to travel a bit."

"How is that going to get me closer to my goal of opening my boutique?"

"For one, it will help you start building your nest egg again. Whether you rely on the money from the bank or not, you still need something to get you started. I think you'll feel more confident if you have consistent income coming in. Since I'm on the partnership team, I'll sort of be your boss."

"And you'll let me pursue my business?"

"You know I won't discourage it, but I'll expect you to get your job done. I know you will."

"I don't know, Tony. It sounds like I might be trading one job in for another one. How is this any different from me working at the agency?"

"For one, Tim wanted you to be a partner. The commitment level for that job is insane. You're running the entire company. There's no way you can be a partner for a company and start another one. Second, he did not want you to pursue your business at all while you were working for him. With our firm, you're not running the entire company, just one division. If you can balance your workload, you can get things running with your business. It's not apples to apples, Talia."

"I suppose you're right." It does sound appealing.

"Think about it," he says as he rises to pay the check for lunch.

"And about moving in with me as well."

"I will."

"Okay, I've got to get back to work. I'll talk to you soon," he leans in to kiss me.

My mind is scrambled as I drive home. Am I ready to move in with Tony? Do I need to take another job just to secure my finances?

I need to pick up a few groceries to cook dinner but decide to check my bank balance before going in.

$233.56.

Wow! It's starting to get real. I need to make some big decisions soon, or Jasmine and I are going to be homeless.

IS IT THE HOBO LIFE FOR TALIA AND JASMINE? FIND OUT ON PAGE 197.

I **pause**. Zack had told me that no matter the decision I made it would require some degree of faith. If I decide to take Tim up on his offer, I'll have to wait longer to launch my business, but I will be able to do it with more resources and with fewer hiccups, if I can trust him. I guess that's where the faith comes in. The old saying goes, "good things come to those who wait." I just need to be patient. I've jumped into this new venture with both feet, without the experience or knowledge of how to move forward. Becoming partner of an advertising agency is a big deal and it will help teach me the business acumen I need to be a successful business owner.

"Well?" Tim is still waiting for my response.

"Yes," I say.

"Yes?"

"Yes, Tim, I will accept your offer to be your partner."

A big smile crawls across his face, reminiscent of the Grinch. I hope I won't live to regret this decision, though the knots forming in my gut tells me I will.

He stands up and reaches across the desk to shake my hand.

"You've made a very wise decision, Talia."

"I hope so."

"You start on Monday."

"Thanks."

I walk down the hallway, hoping I've made the right decision. Allison spots me and quickly ushers me into her office.

"Oh my God, what did you decide? I never heard from you yesterday."

"I know. I didn't want to bother you with my drama. I've been talking your ear off about my situation lately."

"Talia, you're my best friend. You're never a burden! What happened?"

"I came in yesterday and talked to Tim."

"And?"

"He offered me the partnership again."

"Wow, he still left that on the table?"

"Yep."

"Wait, is that what you want? I thought you were tired of the agency life. What about your boutique?"

I sit down in one of the chairs opposite Allison's desk.

"I don't know. I was very discouraged after our visit to the bank. I just realized that I don't know what I'm doing."

"No entrepreneur knows what they're doing in the beginning. They figure it out as they go. Do you think Mr. Stevens knew what he was doing when he first started this agency? You fall down, and you get back up."

"I know, but Tim is willing to help me get back up, so I took him up on his offer."

"At what cost, Talia?" She pleads.

"I work for him as his partner for as long as he needs, and he will invest in my business and help me get started."

"Do you believe he'll make good on his promise?"

"I hope so."

"If that is what you want, I support you, honey. I just want to make sure you don't regret this decision."

"I'm putting my dreams on the back burner for now, but I'm just delaying it for a bit. I'm trading in good for great, and I do believe with Tim's help, I can build something great."

"As long as you're happy," she says, hugging me.

"Well, I've got to go. Kelly is dropping off Jasmine this afternoon after school."

"When do you start?"

"Next Monday."

As I get into my car, I call Tony.

"Hey beautiful!"

"Hi Tony."

"Do you have some news for me?"

I smile.

"I think you'll like it."

"Really?"

"Yes, I decided to take Tim's' offer."

"Wow, I'm surprised. You seemed so against this option last night. What changed your mind?"

"I had some time to think things over and realized that it's okay for me to defer things for a little while if I can capitalize on Tim's expertise to start my business the right way."

"I agree with you. That's all I wanted you to see when we were talking last night. Just know I would have supported you either way."

"I appreciate that. I want you to know that I do still want to open my boutique. That is my dream. Doing this just makes the most sense for what I need right now."

"I support you."

"Thank you."

"Talia, now that this big decision is out of the way, where does that leave us?"

"Why don't you come over later and I'll tell you?"

"I think that can be arranged."

"And, Tony?"

"Yes?"

"Don't forget to bring the ring."

Three years later…

I sit in my office, staring down at my ring. So much has changed. It's hard to believe I was struggling to stay afloat just a few years ago. I took the partnership offer with Tim and he put me to work immediately. I'm on a plane twice a month, meeting with clients and working on new branches where the agency is expanding. Life is crazy.

Tony and I just returned from our honeymoon last week, and the crazy has started all over again. I long to be back on the sandy beaches of Cozumel. Tony's schedule is just as busy as he's recently been promoted to full partner at his architectural firm. Most days, we are like two ships passing in the night. Fortunately, Zack has moved closer and is spending more time with Jasmine, making up for my habitual absence.

"Mrs. Ellison, I just printed your flight itinerary for this afternoon. Should I have the town car pick you up and take you to the airport?"

"Yes, thank you, Janet," I snap back to reality.

As I gather my things, I dial Tony's number.

"Hey there, newlywed," he says.

"Hey yourself. I'm flying to Chicago this evening. There's a mess at the branch and they need my help. I should only be there a couple of days. Can you please touch base with Zack? He should be dropping off Jasmine this evening."

"Of course. She's going to be disappointed that you're not home. She misses you."

"I know, I miss spending time with her, too. Since I took this partner job, I've been traveling nonstop. I'm hoping it will calm down soon, so we can spend some quality time together."

"Have you talked to Tim about opening your boutique?"

"Yea, I've brought it up a couple of times, but he keeps rebuffing me telling me that he's grooming me to be the next CEO of the agency."

"And you're okay with that?"

"I don't know. The more involved I get with this job, the more I realize how much he needs me. Maybe this is my new path."

"You know the most important thing to me is that you're happy."

"I know, baby. I've got to run. They're calling me. I'll call you when I land. Love you."

"Love you, too."

❧

Exhausted, I lean my head against the cool leather of my first-class passenger seat. I hear my neighbor sit down next to me and open my eyes briefly to see who I'll be traveling with.

"Hi, I'm Amber, "she extends her hand.

"Talia," I say, shaking her hand.

"Do you fly much?" she asks.

"Too much," I roll my eyes.

"Really? What do you do, Talia?"

"I'm an executive for an advertising agency."

"That sounds really cool! And they have you doing a lot of traveling, huh? Do you have to go see a lot of clients?"

"Yes, that's part of it. We're also expanding and opening up new branches, so I'm heavily involved in that."

"That sounds like so much fun."

"I do enjoy it. The traveling can get a bit tiring though. Especially since I have a 12-year-old daughter that I'd rather be spending time with."

"I can see how that can be exhausting. I have a 5-year-old – see?" she shows me a picture of her curly-haired little girl.

"My mom lives in Chicago, so I'm traveling there for a few days to get some girl time with her. I'm looking forward to it. I don't travel much but have been pretty busy with work, so I'm glad to have a break to enjoy some family time."

"That's great! What do you do, Amber?" I ask.

"I just opened my own little clothing boutique downtown."

THE END.

"**So how are things** going with the boyfriend?"

I give Zack a buzz to find out what his plans are for moving here. Despite Tony's trepidation, I'm excited to see Zack all the time.

"Things are going. He did not like the idea of you moving in."

"What did I tell you?"

"I know, you were right."

"Do I need to start looking for an apartment?" Zack offers.

"For now, but I don't want to give up on this idea. Zack, I'm running out of money. I don't even know how I'm going to pay my mortgage this month."

"I can pitch in and help you," Zack suggests.

"Tony asked me to move in."

Silence on the line.

"Zack?"

"Wow, that's big."

"I know."

"Did you say yes?"

"I didn't give him my answer yet. I just don't know. Things have been on such shaky ground with us lately, I don't know if we're ready for a move like that."

"Weren't you guys going to get married?" Zack asks.

"Yes, until I called off the engagement. We're back together but taking it slow and I don't know if moving in together is my definition of slow."

"It sounds like you've already made your decision."

"It feels like my life is full of big decisions these days, just so much going on."

"Yeah, but I trust you'll always make the right decision."

"Do you? Do you really think I've made the best decisions, Zack? Be honest. I'm a mother with a child. I had a great paying job with an offer to make more money and have more security. I gave up security for poverty for my own selfish dream. I'm starting to have some regrets."

"There's nothing to regret, Talia. Your dream isn't selfish. You gave up your old life to be a great mother and build a future for Jasmine. You left me and this old town to go to Atlanta to give her what I could never give her at the time. There's nothing wrong with you wanting to go after your dream. This is my opportunity to finally give back to you. I want to support you and help you any way that I can. Don't regret your decision for a minute. Just make good on it."

Now I know why I love him. Wait, what?

A couple weeks pass and I have to close in on a decision with Tony, both to his proposal for moving in and taking the marketing position working at his architectural firm. I humored his suggestion by taking an interview at his company. There was no harm in putting an iron in the fire to expand my options.

Unbeknownst to Tony, Zack loaned me some money to give me a couple more months of oxygen on my living expenses. I have every intention of paying Zack back, so it is no big deal. I just know Tony would get fired up about this since I didn't ask him first. It's fine. Anyway, my interview at Tony's company went quite well. Afterward, Tony told me that the job was a done deal if I wanted it. I received the official offer a week ago. It's a marketing executive role. I would be running the marketing for entire company like Tony said, which means I'd oversee all staff, not just in Atlanta but all branches. There would be some travel involved, not extensive, but maybe every other month to help with campaigns and to run meetings with staff. It's attractive. Not to mention the salary is $150,000 with a very lucrative benefit package. Since I am living off friends, I can't ignore how much this will change my situation. I am still concerned about how much something like this would affect my end goal of starting the boutique. Unlike Tim, Tony has indicated that I am free to get things rolling for my business while working for them which he is in full support of. The job just seems so demanding, I'm not sure I can juggle both. What would be ideal is something part-time that will allow me to bring in enough income while actively working on opening my business somehow. I wonder if that is even possible. Either way, my deadline is tomorrow, and I am having dinner with Tony tonight to let him know my decision – on everything.

I'm not going to agonize over that now. Right now, I'm enjoying some one on one girl time with my bestie.

Allison and I meet at one of our favorite little cafés downtown.

"Hey stranger!" she yells as she runs up to me and gives me a big hug.

It has only been a couple of weeks, but it really does feel like we haven't talked in forever.

"It's so good to see you. I've missed you," I give her a big hug.

"Well, you've had a lot going on."

"Tell me about it."

"That's what I hoping you'll do," Allison grabs her seat. The waiter comes over, takes our drink orders, and gives us our menus.

"Tomorrow's the deadline, right, for the big marketing job?"

"Yes, what do you think?" I ask.

"It's a very good offer. There's no question about that. Tony works for one of the best architectural firms not just in Atlanta, but the country. In all honesty, this may be even bigger than the agency gig even though you were offered partner there. This company is bigger, Tal."

"I know. They're international. You think I should take it?"

Allison leans back, playing with the napkin in her lap.

"I didn't say that."

"What are you saying?"

"I'm saying you need to listen to your heart, Tal. You need to do what feels right. Do you still want to open your store?"

"You know I do."

"Then, everything decision you make needs to filter through that."

I bury my head in my face on the table.

"Allison, that's what I've been trying to do. But, I have yet to see where these big decisions I'm making are paying off. I'm broke with no real money coming in. The money I'm making working at this retail shop is a joke. If it weren't for Zack, I'd probably be homeless right now."

"So, take Tony up on his offer to move in, or have Zack move in. Have you made a decision on that yet?"

"No."

Allison places a reassuring hand on my wrist.

"Tal, what do you want?"

"I want things to get easier."

She laughs. My tension eases for moment and I laugh with her.

"You know that's not going to happen, right?"

"A girl can dream, can't she?"

"And you do, Tal. It's what I love so much about you. I know things are crazy right now, but I admire you so much for going after what you want. Without even realizing it, you have accomplished so much already."

"How?"

"By doing what most people would be afraid to do. You gave up an incredible job opportunity after working your ass off to get where you were, to go down an uncertain road with this business…."

"I don't know how admirable that is," I interject.

"You didn't let me finish, Tal. It's uncertain because it's new to you. I didn't say you wouldn't make it. I do believe you will make this work – if you want to. You're so brave. You feel in your heart that this is your dream, and you're going for it."

"I have no idea what I'm doing."

"That's okay. Just find someone who does. Let them guide you."

"How do I do that?"

"Always be looking. When you know what you want, the pieces come together, I promise you."

We enjoy our lunch together, then decide to take a stroll downtown to browse some of the local shops.

"This place is new," I point to a cute boutique that has just popped up in the area.

"Let's go in, "Allison says.

As we browse, I realize this place has nearly everything I've envisioned for my own boutique. It is perfect.

"Are you finding everything okay?"

I turn around to see a young woman smiling.

"Yes, thank you. Is this place new? My friend and I haven't seen it around here before?"

"Brand new," the young woman beams, "we just had our grand opening a few days ago."

"Your place is beautiful," I compliment her. "Whoever designed it place has remarkable taste. It's everything I ever envisioned."

"Do you have a store of your own?" the girl queries.

"No, not yet," I say, "but I'd like to open a place like this someday."

"It's been a journey, I'll tell you. It's taken a while for all of the pieces to come together but, I'm pleased to finally see my vision alive before me."

"I'm Amber," the young girl says, extending her hand, "I'm the owner of this place."

Allison walks up as Amber is introducing herself.

"Hi, I'm Allison and this is my friend Talia. Did I just hear you say you were the owner of this place?"

"Yes, I did."

"Talia has been trying to get things going for her own shop. I know we just met, but any chance we can get together and grab coffee sometime? I know she'd love any insight you can offer her on how to get going."

"Of course," Amber grins "the life of a business owner is quite unpredictable. Making the decision to start a boutique is a commitment. Talia, what made you want to open your own store? Do you have a background in fashion?"

I frown.

"Not exactly. I have a background in marketing and advertising, but I have always loved fashion. This has been a dream of mine since I was in high school. I just realized now that it's what I want to do."

"Wow, marketing and advertising, that's a valuable skill set. I may have to pick your brain a bit. After all, you can't run a successful store without a good marketing plan. I'd love to get your insight on some things as well. I have a background in fashion design. It's what I studied in college. I carry a few of my designs here in the store. After I graduated, I worked in retail for almost ten years before I realized I was ready to be the one in charge. I worked my way high up the ranks in management, but when you work for large corporations, you're never in control, even as a manager. I realized the only way I'd gain full creative control and get my designs out there was to create the opportunity myself. And, that's how this place was born."

"How did you get this going while working a busy job in retail?" I'm so curious to learn more about this girl who is living my dream.

About that time, several more people walk into the store. Amber sees that her attention is needed.

"It looks like we're going to need to have that coffee," she says. She reaches in her pocket, pulls out a card, and writes a number on the back.

"Here's my card. I wrote my cell number on the back. Give me a call and we can set something up. I'm sure there's a lot we can learn from each other."

"Thank you," I say with a big smile on my face.

"No problem. I've got to take care of these customers but if you see anything you like or have any other questions about the merchandise, just grab me."

Then, she is off to greet her new customers.

"Did that just happen?" I ask my friend.

"What did I tell you?"

"If it weren't for you, I don't even know if I would have said anything. Thanks Allison."

"What are friends for? Guard that card with your life. This girl has got the secret," Allison admires our surroundings. It's a beautiful store.

We leave the shop and continue our walk. I carefully tuck Amber's card into my purse. It is my newest treasure.

"It seems you have a lot to figure out," Allison says.

"Story of my life."

"Are you going to take the job?"

"I haven't figured that out yet. No matter what I decide on the job, I have a feeling Amber is the key to getting unstuck."

"I agree with you, my friend. I'm a firm believer that there are no such things are coincidences. Don't take this meeting with Amber for granted."

I hold tight onto my purse that protects Amber's precious card.

"I won't."

I am getting ready for dinner with Tony when Jasmine peers into my bedroom. Meeting Amber has been a breaking point in this entire process. Now, I've got to be proactive in doing something about this chance encounter.

"You look pretty, Mommy."

"Thank you, sweetheart."

"Mommy?"

"Yes, baby."

"Are you still going to start that store you told me about? With the clothes?"

If anyone can keep me accountable to my dreams, it is this precious girl. She never forgets anything.

"Mommy's working on it, baby."

"I hope you do it."

"Yeah? Why?"

"I want some free clothes."

I laugh. A child after my own heart. She is definitely mine.

"I'll see what I can do about that. In the meantime, go back to your room and make sure you've finished up your homework. The sitter will be here soon. She brought a movie for you to watch after you eat dinner."

"A movie?" Jasmine asks excitedly, "what movie?"

"You'll have to ask her, but I'm pretty sure it's one you've been wanting to see. You won't be able to watch anything if your homework isn't done. Now, go."

Jasmine runs down the hall to finish her homework, while I work on the finishing touches of my makeup. Tony should be here any minute.

Ding-dong. Right on time! That's either the babysitter or Tony.

I run downstairs to find my handsome boyfriend on the other side of the door.

"Well, aren't you a vision?" He leans in to give me a kiss, and hands me a beautiful bouquet of red roses.

"What are these for?"

"Just because."

I smile at his romantic gesture. We've been on such rocky

ground the last few months that it is nice to see his romantic side coming back.

"As soon as Jasmine's sitter gets here, we can go."

"Okay," Tony says as he takes a seat in the kitchen. "Have you made your decision about the job yet?"

"I knew you were going to ask me that."

"The deadline is tomorrow."

"Yes, it is, but I thought we'd reserve that conversation for dinner."

Ding-dong. Saved by the bell.

I run to the door to let the sitter in, give her all the instructions for Jasmine, and then run back to Tony.

"Ready?"

"You're the best at evading questions," he chuckles, "but it's okay. Like you said, we can discuss at dinner."

As we ride to the restaurant, I start to feel anxious. I don't want to make the wrong decision. There is so much on the line.

We have a wonderful dinner. We laugh and joke together which is something we haven't done in a while. Things feel normal again.

Tony reaches across the table and squeezes my hand.

"It's been a long time since we've been like this."

"I know," I smile.

"It's nice."

"I agree."

"I know you've had a lot on your mind lately. There's the job offer from the firm. I think it's such a great fit for you, Talia, and I do think you can still make your plans for your boutique if you are judicious with your time. I can't wait to hear what you've decided. There is one other thing I want to add to your plate, but I'm hoping it's a good thing."

Tony gets down on one knee, in front of the entire restaurant.

"Talia Cooper, I love you so much. You're the best thing that has ever happened to me. Our relationship has been a roller coaster the last few months with all the changes you have been going through.

But, through all of it, my feelings for you haven't changed. A couple weeks ago, I asked you to move in with me, and I realized that the only way to show you how serious I am about our relationship, and you, is to put this ring back on your finger. So, Talia Cooper, will you be my wife?"

YOU LOVE TONY. ACCEPT HIS PROPOSAL, TAKE THE JOB AT HIS FIRM AND START YOUR LIFE TOGETHER. IT'S A MEANS TO AN END. TURN TO PAGE 208.

BREAK TONY'S HEART AND TURN DOWN HIS PROPOSAL AND HIS JOB AT HIS FIRM. YOUR DREAM HAS BEEN ON THE SHELF TOO LONG. TURN TO THE NEXT PAGE.

I stand there, frozen. I can't speak.

"Talia?"

Everyone in the room is looking me expectantly.

"Tony, can I speak to you alone please?"

I guide him outside the restaurant where there isn't an audience waiting for my answer.

"What's wrong, Talia?"

"I can't accept your proposal."

"Why?"

"I don't think we're ready for this kind of commitment. I love you, but I just don't know if I want to marry you right now."

Tony closes the ring box and rolls his eyes.

"Please tell me Zack doesn't have anything to do with this."

"This isn't about Zack. It's about how we seem to just be on separate paths right now. We've tried to make this work, but it feels like we just keep band-aiding the issue."

"I guess that means that you are turning down my firm's job offer as well."

I nod.

"It's not what I need right now."

"Oh my God! You've got to be kidding me! Talia, you have no money!"

"Just tell the whole damn city, Tony! Geez, can you take me home please?"

"Just answer this for me – how is the job not on your path?"

"I can't see how I can start my boutique and work this job at the same time. It's really demanding and there is not going to be any room for me to do what I need to do."

Tony grabs me by the shoulders like he was trying to shake some sense into me.

"Talia, listen to me. For your own good, let this boutique crap go! It is ruining your life. You are letting the best opportunities of your life pass you by for what? A whim?"

I shake out of his grasp.

"Wow," I say quietly, "tell me how you really feel."

We get in the car and ride back to my home in silence.

As I get out the car and walk to the door, Tony calls out.

"Talia, what does this mean for us? Are we done?"

I look at my lost love through teary eyes.

"I think you know the answer," and I walk into the house without another word.

Tony and I have been on a wild ride the last couple of months, but something about this feels definitive. He isn't coming back, and I'm not going to be forgiving of his remarks.

I want to call Zack. He's been there every time I've been upset in the last few months. Then, I realize that he is coming in town tomorrow. I am done imposing on him at late hours of the night. I expect to cry myself to sleep, but the tears don't come. I suspect I've used up all the tears I'm going to shed over Tony. Instead, I can't wait to see Zack tomorrow.

Go to page 212 to pick up Zack.

Tears well up in my eyes. I love him, and we've been through so much in the last few months. He is everything I ever wanted and envisioned in a man. Together, we make the perfect couple. Jasmine loves him, too. This is the right decision.

"Yes," I say, hugging and kissing him, "yes."

"You've made the me happiest man in the world," he whispers against my lips.

"I'm pretty happy, too."

"And, the job?"

"Yes."

"Yes?"

"Yes, I'll take the job."

Tony picks me up and spins me around.

"We are going to have such a great life together. I promise you."

"I believe you."

❧

Jasmine is already in bed when I return home so I decide to tell her big news tomorrow. I look down at the princess diamond on my finger. I am getting married. There is one person I want to tell.

"Hello."

"Zack?"

"Did I wake you?"

"By now, I'm used to your calls at night? Although 10:30 is pretty early for you."

I snicker.

"I have news."

"Good news?"

"I like to think it is."

"Okay."

"Tony and I just got engaged."

"Wow, that is big. Are you guys ready for that step?"

"I think so. These last few months have been a little rocky, but I do love him. Yes, we're ready for this."

"You don't have to convince me. If you're happy, you know I'm happy."

"I also decided to take that job."

"Really?"

"Yes."

"You don't think it will be too much."

"It's an undertaking, but I met a girl today. She owns a boutique downtown. She just opened it and she is willing to grab coffee with me. I'm hoping to learn some things from her that can help me figure out how to get started."

"Well, at least you have a plan. That's progress, and the job does fix your finances."

"Yes, and I can pay you back."

"Talia, you don't have to pay me back."

"I want to."

"You're the mother of my child. I'll always support you any way I can."

I'll always have a tender disposition toward Zack. He is so special to me.

"There's something else."

"Okay."

"Tony asked me to move in with him."

"Wow, you guys are making all of your big decisions at once."

"Yes. I mean, we're getting married now, so we'll be moving in together anyway."

"Makes sense."

"So that leaves the townhouse."

"Yeah?"

"Well, you'll be here for your new job in the next couple of weeks. You need a place to stay. I already offered you a bedroom to stay in. How do you feel about renting the townhouse from me?"

"Really?"

"If I'm moving in with Tony, what am I going to do with it? Plus, it can still be home for Jasmine. We can figure out the expenses. For now, I know you need a place, so why not stay here?"

"That's a generous offer, Tal. As long as you're sure?"

"Yes, I'm sure."

"Okay."

"Zack?"

"Thank you so much for supporting me through all of this."

"Anytime."

※

Running to grab a quick lunch with Allison, it's hard to believe that I've been working at the firm with Tony for a year now. The last year has been a whirlwind. Zack moved to Atlanta and started living in the townhouse. I moved in with Tony and took the marketing executive job at his firm. Life is fast and furious. On top of everything, I am planning a wedding that is now just two weeks away! Allison is my maid of honor and we're working out some wedding details over lunch.

"Hey sweetie," Allison greets me, "how's life?"

"Crazy busy. This job has been one thing after another since I took it."

"Are you having fun?"

"Kinda."

"Kinda?"

"I'm in familiar territory. The environment is not the same as the agency, but in a good way. I have more creative control. They just trust me to do what's best and that is very freeing."

"That's good. What about the boutique? Did you ever have coffee with that girl? What's her name?"

What is her name?

"Yes, I remember her. I saved her card." I rifle through my purse but find no sign of the card that I'd held so tight my breast a year ago. "I can't find it."

"Maybe you can stop by her shop and get her information again."

"Do you think she'd even remember me? I can't even remember her name."

"I don't know. She might."

"Maybe, but honestly Allison, I don't know where I'll fit in the time to open a boutique right now. Between the wedding, this job and trying to be a good mom to Jasmine, who has time for that?"

"Your plate is pretty full."

"It really is. I guess this will just have to take a backseat right now until the time feels right again."

THE END.

I meet Zack for lunch when he gets into town.

As Zack takes a bite of his burger, he senses something is wrong.

"What happened last night? You had to make your big decision on the job and everything, right?"

I can't hold it in any longer. The tears start steaming.

"Zack…"

I can't find my words.

"That bad, huh?"

"Tony proposed."

Zack rakes me over skeptically.

"This is not usually the reaction a guy goes for when he proposes."

I stifle a laugh through my tears.

"I know. I wasn't expecting him to propose. I wasn't ready for it. I just couldn't say yes, Zack."

"Do you love him?"

"I thought I did."

"Thought?"

"We've been together about a year. Things were going so well, and when we hit our first resistance, we didn't rebound well. Our philosophies are so different. He can't see things through my eyes and just can't support what I want to do with my boutique. He told me last night point blank to give it up. He called it a whim. He said I was ruining my life!"

I pick up my napkin to wipe my eyes.

"Wow," Zack says, placing his hand over mine, gently.

"I guess I can see why you're so upset now. I'm sorry that you're going through this."

"Hey, it's better that I figure it out now, instead of after I marry the guy."

"True."

"Thanks for listening to me ramble, Zack. You are the only one who truly understands me."

"And that has taken years," he says, chuckling.

I love how comfortable we are with each other.

"Are you ready to look at some apartments?" He asks.

"About that…"

"What?" Zack asks, sounding anxious.

"How do you feel about taking me up on my original proposal?"

"What? To stay with you and Jasmine?"

"Yes."

"I thought Tony hated that idea."

"It looks like Tony is a non-factor right now."

"You don't want to be presumptuous, Tal. Your wounds are fresh. What if you guys can fix this and end up getting back together? I don't want to get in the way of that."

"Have you heard anything I've been telling you? Tony and I are going in opposite directions. You can't build a solid foundation on that. We're on rocky ground. As much as it hurts, we're not getting back together."

"Tal, I don't know."

"Jasmine would love to have you under the same roof. Plus, you'd still be helping me out financially, since I just turned down another huge job offer."

Zack pauses a moment to think.

"Sure, why not? We can try it and see if it works. I can always get a place somewhere else if it doesn't. This is just meant to be temporary, right?"

"Right."

૮હ

Tony made many attempts to get back in my good graces over the last couple of weeks but after I ignore enough of his calls, he gets the message that I am done this time. Zack is moving into the townhouse and getting ready to start his new job and I am working on dinner downstairs.

My purse falls the floor and as I pick it up, a business card slips out.

It's Amber's card, the boutique shop owner I'd met about a few weeks ago. We are supposed to be getting together for coffee. I turn the card over, and Amber's hand-written cell number is there. I dial the number.

"Hello Amber?"

"Yes, this is Amber."

"Amber, I don't know if you remember me. I'm Talia. My friend Allison and I were in your shop about a few weeks ago, right after you opened, and I shared with you that I wanted to open a shop of my own and that I had a background in marketing and advertising."

"Yes, I remember you! I was hoping that you'd call me. I realized after you left that I gave you my card, but I never got your number. I'd really like to pick your brain on some marketing ideas for my business. Do you want to grab that coffee?"

"Absolutely!"

We put a date on the calendar to grab coffee at a local café the following week.

Zack walks into the kitchen to grab a bottle of water just as I am hanging up the phone.

"Is that the last of it?" I ask.

"Yep, just got the last of my things in my room. What are you smiling so hard about?"

"Remember that girl that owns that downtown boutique I told you about? The one I wanted to grab coffee with?"

"I think I remember you telling me about her."

"I just got off the phone with her. We are getting together for coffee next week. I'm so excited!"

"That's great," Zack takes a seat at the kitchen table to finish his water.

"What's your plan with her?"

"I'm hoping to learn some ideas from her on how to get my store off the ground."

"Didn't you say the bank lender told you that you needed a partner to get approved for a loan? Someone with experience in the industry?"

"Yes."

"Do you think she might be willing to partner with you to get your store off the ground?"

"I don't know, Zack. At this point, we're still strangers. She doesn't know me well enough to invest in a partnership with me."

Zack shrugs.

"I'm saying…it just never hurts to ask."

"I guess you're right."

"Have you talked to Tony? It's been a couple weeks now."

I pull up a chair to sit at the kitchen table with Zack.

"Why are you so interested in my love life?"

Zack laughs.

"I didn't say I was that interested. I just want you to be happy, that's all."

"Why?"

"Why? Talia, you know why. You're Jasmine's mother. We share a child together. I'll always care about you."

"Mmm."

"Mmm? What's that mean?"

"I was just wondering…"

"Wondering what?"

I've managed a perfect relationship with Zack over the years. He is my best friend. I don't want to wreck that, but these feelings have been bubbling beneath the surface for a while now. It's time to get some clarity.

"Wondering if it's a little bit more."

"More?"

"A few weeks ago, we were on the phone. One of our many late-night conversations. Before you hung up, you said, 'you know I love you.'"

"Yea…and?"

"Zack, you said you loved me."

"Tal, that's no mystery. You were my first love. I'll always love you. Where is all of this coming from?"

I lower my head, searching my heart for the feelings I know are already there.

"I was…I was just wondering if maybe I feel the same."

"Of course, you do. We've always had something special, Tal," he says, grabbing my hand, "we're best friends."

"Nothing more?" I ask.

"What?"

I get up and walk away from Zack.

"Tal, what are you talking about?"

"I can't help but wonder if one of the reasons I could not commit fully to Tony is because I still have feelings for you."

"Tal, I think you are confusing your feelings. It's been a long time since we were a couple. And, we were kids."

"Yes, we were. But, Zack, no one knows me the way you do. I feel a comfort with you that I've never felt with anyone else. Not even Tony. And, we've both grown a lot together over the years."

Silence.

"Don't tell me you have never thought about it…you and me."

Zack laughs.

"Of course, I've thought about it. Countless times. If you remember, you left me, not the other way around. Then, you started dating Mr. Perfect. How was I supposed to compete with that?"

"You weren't."

We lock eyes for a moment, remembering the young love that conceived our daughter.

I walk over to Zack, grab his hands, and hold them in my own.

"I thought I had everything figured out. I moved here, worked my butt off and created the career I thought I'd always wanted, earning money I never dreamed of, and meeting the man of my dreams. Now, I realize that I never needed any of those things. Everything that I ever needed was right here all along, and I was just too stupid to see it. I have clarity for the first time in my life. Not just about my career goals, but my life – with you."

Zack gently caresses my face, and my cheeks warm at his touch.

"Are you sure this is what you want?"

"Do you love me?"

His expression tells me there's no question.

"You know I do."

"Then, yes. With you by side, I feel like I can conquer the world. I need you, Zack."

"Okay," he says as he pulls me in for a long-awaited kiss. Eight years of deferred love, and we feel it.

Zack pulls away from our passionate embrace as we both catch our breath.

"So, this is it, we're going to be a family?" He asks.

I plant baby kisses on Zack's lips, excited to rekindle our love.

"Yes."

"Does this mean I get to move into the master bedroom now?"

I stroke Zack's hair teasingly.

"Patience makes the heart grow fonder, sir."

"I think I've been patient long enough," Zack whispers in my ear as he hoists me over his shoulders and runs up the stairs.

I sit in the quaint, little coffee shop, a smile painting my lips. Things have been hectic the last few months. I've been trying to figure out my career goals, but things finally seem to be falling in place. Zack has moved in, and now that he is a little more than a roommate, our trio really feels like a family. Jasmine has never been happier with both of her parents under the same roof. Zack took charge of the finances immediately to help relieve the pressure I was feeling after leaving my job. I recently found a part-time job doing marketing for a small boutique agency. Though it is not a fashion related position, it allows me to manage a flexible schedule so that I can work on building my store while having a consistent income to complement what Zack is earning. I am excited about meeting with Amber so that we can brainstorm ideas to get my business off the ground.

Lost in my thoughts, I don't even see Amber walk in.

"Talia?"

"Oh, hi Amber. Sorry, I guess I was daydreaming."

"It's okay," she laughs, "I find myself doing that all the time. I'm so glad we were able to do this."

"Me too!"

"Where should we start? I have to tell you, I have so many questions and things I want to pick your brain on."

"That's good, because I have the same for you. I'm hoping that we'll be able to help each other quite a bit."

"Good! Why don't you start?" She offers.

"Okay, well you know that I want to start my own boutique."

"Yes, I remember you telling me that."

"I kind of had an epiphany a few months ago and made some pretty drastic life decisions once I realized that I wanted to do this. I quit my job. Not something I'd really planned but my boss approached me with an offer to be a partner, which would require a ridiculous time commitment. I didn't see how I could make that work and build a business at the same time, so I turned him down along with a large salary – twice. "

"Wow, that was a bold move."

"Tell me about it. A lot of people thought I was crazy to walk away from that kind of stability and the opportunity to run an agency on that level, especially since I have a little girl. Am I crazy?"

Amber laughs.

"No, Talia, you're not crazy. You're an entrepreneur. You can't accomplish anything extraordinary in your life if you continue to fall in step with what everyone else wants you to do. I commend you for what you did. It was brave."

"Thank you for helping to validate my decision, because I have no idea what I'm doing. I drafted up a business plan and have started to map out how I want things to look. I went to the bank to try to get funding and they turned me down point blank. They said I didn't have enough experience and suggested that I get some experience in the industry or get a partner and come back in a year."

"First mistake - never go to bank first. That's always discouraging."

"Didn't you have to get funding to open your store?" I ask, a little confused.

"Eventually."

"Please go on."

"I told you that I worked in retail before I started my store, and you know how hectic that can be."

"Yes, I do."

"I started my store incrementally. I started with accessories, then I slowly started to add more design pieces, including my own. I started to build relationships with manufacturers."

"But you just opened your store?"

"I just opened my brick and mortar space. I've been online for five years."

"Oooh."

Things are starting to come into focus.

"I want to tell you that you're thinking too big, Talia. But, that's not what I mean. Thinking big is great. You need a big vision for what you want your business to look like. But you don't need to do everything at once. Bite off small pieces at a time. It allows you to learn more as you go and invest less money as well."

"That makes so much sense, Amber. I've been putting way too much pressure on myself trying to get everything in place to physically open a store."

"Yes, you have. Start with building an online presence. With your marketing background, I'd think that piece would be a breeze for you."

"Marketing does come easily to me. I could use your help navigating the waters of building relationships with manufacturers and distributors."

"I'm happy to help you. As a matter of fact, I have a proposition for you."

"I'll coach you on getting your business started, if you you'll coach me on my marketing and advertising. That way we can capitalize on each other's expertise so both businesses can grow. What do you think?"

"I think you've got a deal."

"Great. Let me make sure I have all your information this time. I want to send you some information on next steps. And, can we set up another meeting, so I can share my marketing plan with you and get your feedback and suggestions?"

"Of course!"

I walk out of the coffee shop confidently. The tide in my life has shifted. Though everything isn't in place yet, for the first time in months, I have a firm plan for next steps. I know what I want and what I need to do to get there. I'm not alone. My support team is amazing. Zack has been my rock along with Jasmine, Allison and now, my new friend, Amber. I am on a roll. Nothing is stopping me now.

THE END.

ABOUT THE AUTHOR

Nakita has been writing since the age of 13. She has always been fascinated with the art of storytelling and working with others to find their own story within. She was inspired to write *The Decision* to help others realize the impact to pursuing their dreams, while educating them on the calculated risks involved in the process.

An author, ghostwriter and writing coach, Nakita continues to inspire others to live their best lives and tell their unique stories to impact and influence.

www.ingramcontent.com/pod-product-compliance
Lightning Source LLC
Chambersburg PA
CBHW071413070526
44578CB00003B/565